STERLING BIOGRAPHIES

# JACKIE ROBINSON

## Champion for Equality

Michael Teitelbaum

STERLING

New York / London
www.sterlingpublishing.com/kids

I would like to thank my buddy Jim Buckley of the Shoreline Publishing Group for steering this project my way; my editor at Sterling, Susan Schader, for her patience and editorial guidance; and my wife, Sheleigah, for sitting next to me at all the Mets games.

This book is dedicated to Sharon Robinson for her kindness, generosity, and passion for her father's legacy, all of which inspired me as a writer and thrilled me as a baseball fan.

STERLING and the distinctive Sterling logo are registered trademarks of
Sterling Publishing Co., Inc.

**Library of Congress Cataloging-in-Publication Data**
Teitelbaum, Michael.
  Jackie Robinson : champion for equality / Michael Teitelbaum.
      p. cm. — (Sterling biographies)
  Includes bibliographical references and index.
  ISBN 978-1-4027-6362-5 (pbk.) — ISBN 978-1-4027-7148-4 (hardcover) 1. Robinson, Jackie,
1919–1972—Juvenile literature. 2. Baseball players—United States—Biography—Juvenile
literature. 3. African American baseball players—Biography—Juvenile literature. I. Title.
  GV865.R6T45 2010
  796.357092—dc22
  [B]
                                                                            2009024219

Lot #: 10  9  8  7  6  5  4  3  2  1
12/09

Published by Sterling Publishing Co., Inc.
387 Park Avenue South, New York, NY 10016
© 2010 by Michael Teitelbaum

Distributed in Canada by Sterling Publishing
c/o Canadian Manda Group, 165 Dufferin Street
Toronto, Ontario, Canada M6K 3H6
Distributed in the United Kingdom by GMC Distribution Services
Castle Place, 166 High Street, Lewes, East Sussex, England BN7 1XU
Distributed in Australia by Capricorn Link (Australia) Pty. Ltd.
P.O. Box 704, Windsor, NSW 2756, Australia

*Printed in China*
*All rights reserved*

Sterling ISBN 978-1-4027-7148-4 (hardcover)
          ISBN 978-1-4027-6362-5 (paperback)

Image research by Jim Gigliotti and James Buckley, Jr.

For information about custom editions, special sales, premium and corporate
purchases, please contact Sterling Special Sales Department at 800-805-5489
or specialsales@sterlingpublishing.com.

# Contents

# Events in the Life of Jackie Robinson

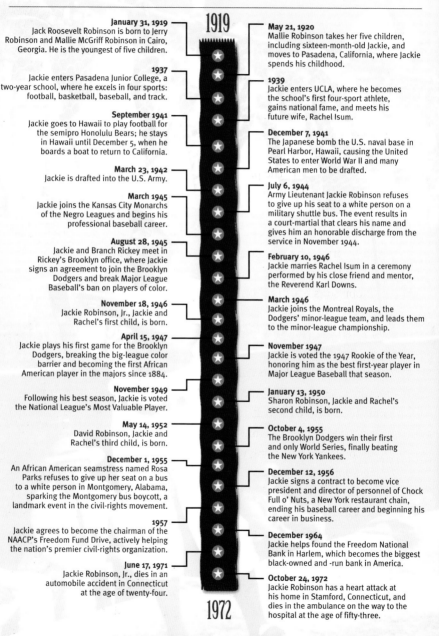

**1919**

**January 31, 1919**
Jack Roosevelt Robinson is born to Jerry Robinson and Mallie McGriff Robinson in Cairo, Georgia. He is the youngest of five children.

**May 21, 1920**
Mallie Robinson takes her five children, including sixteen-month-old Jackie, and moves to Pasadena, California, where Jackie spends his childhood.

**1937**
Jackie enters Pasadena Junior College, a two-year school, where he excels in four sports: football, basketball, baseball, and track.

**1939**
Jackie enters UCLA, where he becomes the school's first four-sport athlete, gains national fame, and meets his future wife, Rachel Isum.

**September 1941**
Jackie goes to Hawaii to play football for the semipro Honolulu Bears; he stays in Hawaii until December 5, when he boards a boat to return to California.

**December 7, 1941**
The Japanese bomb the U.S. naval base in Pearl Harbor, Hawaii, causing the United States to enter World War II and many American men to be drafted.

**March 23, 1942**
Jackie is drafted into the U.S. Army.

**July 6, 1944**
Army Lieutenant Jackie Robinson refuses to give up his seat to a white person on a military shuttle bus. The event results in a court-martial that clears his name and gives him an honorable discharge from the service in November 1944.

**March 1945**
Jackie joins the Kansas City Monarchs of the Negro Leagues and begins his professional baseball career.

**August 28, 1945**
Jackie and Branch Rickey meet in Rickey's Brooklyn office, where Jackie signs an agreement to join the Brooklyn Dodgers and break Major League Baseball's ban on players of color.

**February 10, 1946**
Jackie marries Rachel Isum in a ceremony performed by his close friend and mentor, the Reverend Karl Downs.

**March 1946**
Jackie joins the Montreal Royals, the Dodgers' minor-league team, and leads them to the minor-league championship.

**November 18, 1946**
Jackie Robinson, Jr., Jackie and Rachel's first child, is born.

**April 15, 1947**
Jackie plays his first game for the Brooklyn Dodgers, breaking the big-league color barrier and becoming the first African American player in the majors since 1884.

**November 1947**
Jackie is voted the 1947 Rookie of the Year, honoring him as the best first-year player in Major League Baseball that season.

**November 1949**
Following his best season, Jackie is voted the National League's Most Valuable Player.

**January 13, 1950**
Sharon Robinson, Jackie and Rachel's second child, is born.

**May 14, 1952**
David Robinson, Jackie and Rachel's third child, is born.

**October 4, 1955**
The Brooklyn Dodgers win their first and only World Series, finally beating the New York Yankees.

**December 1, 1955**
An African American seamstress named Rosa Parks refuses to give up her seat on a bus to a white person in Montgomery, Alabama, sparking the Montgomery bus boycott, a landmark event in the civil-rights movement.

**December 12, 1956**
Jackie signs a contract to become vice president and director of personnel of Chock Full o' Nuts, a New York restaurant chain, ending his baseball career and beginning his career in business.

**1957**
Jackie agrees to become the chairman of the NAACP's Freedom Fund Drive, actively helping the nation's premier civil-rights organization.

**December 1964**
Jackie helps found the Freedom National Bank in Harlem, which becomes the biggest black-owned and -run bank in America.

**June 17, 1971**
Jackie Robinson, Jr., dies in an automobile accident in Connecticut at the age of twenty-four.

**October 24, 1972**
Jackie Robinson has a heart attack at his home in Stamford, Connecticut, and dies in the ambulance on the way to the hospital at the age of fifty-three.

**1972**

# Stealing Home

*Above anything else, I hate to lose.*

The runner on third base dashed down the third-base line toward home plate. Then he stopped and darted back toward the third-base **bag**, as if daring the pitcher to try and throw him out. The pitcher removed his cap, wiped the sweat from his brow, and stared hard at the runner.

The runner was Jackie Robinson of the National League champion Brooklyn Dodgers. The pitcher was Whitey Ford of the American League champion New York Yankees. This was Game One of the 1955 World Series.

Robinson's blazing speed was well known, as was his love of **stealing** home. Again, he danced down the third-base line. Ford began his windup, ready to throw his pitch.

That's when Robinson took off, head down, arms pumping, feet pounding the dirt. He was trying to reach home plate before the ball got there. The pitch slammed into catcher Yogi Berra's mitt with an explosive crack.

Robinson slid, kicking up clouds of dust. Berra tried to tag Robinson before his foot touched home plate.

"Safe!" the umpire shouted, when the dust finally cleared.

Jackie Robinson had stolen home, not only scoring a run for the Brooklyn Dodgers, but also tossing another brick at the barrier of racial injustice in America's national pastime—a barrier he had broken eight years earlier when he took his first steps onto a **Major League Baseball** field.

# CHAPTER 1

# Humble Beginnings

*My grandfather was born into slavery, and my mother and father lived in a newer, more sophisticated kind of slavery than the kind Mr. Lincoln struck down.*

Jackie Robinson has become a symbol of the fight for social justice and the battle to end racial **segregation** and **discrimination** in America. But his is still a personal story.

He simply wanted a chance in life, the same chance that white people had in the land of the free—to forge a life based on his abilities, his character, and his intellect, rather than on the color of his skin. This may not sound like such a radical idea today, but in the America into which Jackie Robinson was born, it was little more than a fanciful dream.

Jack Roosevelt Robinson was born on January 31, 1919, in the rural northern Georgia town of Cairo. Like the rest of the South at that time, the town was dominated by the segregated government policies known as Jim Crow laws.

The Jim Crow laws prevented black people from using the same restaurants, hotels, schools, parks, buses, swimming pools, bathrooms, and water fountains that white people did. Although slavery had been **abolished** in the United States more than fifty years earlier, Jim Crow

Jim Crow laws in the South made segregation legal. This undated photograph shows separate drinking fountains for whites and blacks.

laws made black people second-class citizens who did not enjoy the freedoms and opportunities white Americans had.

Jackie Robinson's grandparents had been slaves. His parents, Jerry and Mallie (McGriff) Robinson, were sharecroppers, in a system that Jackie later called "a newer, more sophisticated kind of slavery than the kind Mr. Lincoln struck down."

Sharecropping was a system of farming that developed in Georgia in the 1860s following the end of slavery and spread throughout the South. Under this system, laborers who did not own land worked on farm plots owned by someone else in exchange for a portion of the crops they grew. In Georgia, the landowners were mostly white farmers. The sharecroppers, also known as tenant farmers, were most often black.

Jackie and his four older siblings (three brothers and a sister) were born into poverty. They lived in a run-down shack on the **plantation** where Jerry and Mallie Robinson worked as sharecroppers. Jerry and Mallie were caught in an unfair situation. They worked very hard to farm land owned by someone else in return for very little food.

The year that Jackie was born, his father, fed up with the hard work for little reward, abandoned the family, leaving Mallie Robinson to raise five children by herself—nine-year-old Edgar, eight-year-old Frank, five-year-old Mack, three-year-old Willa Mae, and six-month-old Jackie.

# Jim Crow Laws

Although federal law ended slavery in 1865, local and state laws calling for "separate but equal" facilities for whites and nonwhites were still allowed. In reality, while these facilities were separate, they were far from equal. Black people had to put up with inadequate, inferior facilities when it came to schools, restaurants, housing, and public transportation. The Jim Crow laws, named for an offensive black character from an 1800s song, maintained many of the injustices of slavery.

These laws were also used to deny black people their constitutionally guaranteed right to vote. Poll taxes (charging people a fee to vote) and literacy requirements (being able to read) kept blacks from voting. These laws denied them the ability to elect officials who could represent them and work to get rid of the Jim Crow laws.

In the twentieth century, landmark U.S. Supreme Court cases began to chip away at these laws. In *Morgan v. Commonwealth of Virginia* (1946), the court ruled that segregation in interstate transportation was unconstitutional. *Brown v. Board of Education of Topeka* (1954) did away with school segregation.

This is the original verdict in the landmark U.S. Supreme Court case *Brown v. Board of Education of Topeka*. The court ruled on May 17, 1954, that school segregation was unconstitutional.

The Civil Rights Act of 1964 and the Voting Rights Act of 1965 finally did away with all Jim Crow laws in the United States.

Jackie's parents were sharecroppers in Georgia. A typical sharecropper's home looked like this one from the 1930s.

Mallie's strength alone held her young family together. Her belief in honesty, the importance of family, and her strong religious beliefs guided her through the incredibly difficult task of being a single black mother in the South, which was dominated by Jim Crow laws. For the rest of his life, Jackie Robinson would always credit his mother's love, strength, and guidance as the reason he grew into the man he became.

A chance visit by Mallie's half-brother, Burton Thomas, provided a way out of the family's terrible situation. Burton lived in Pasadena, California, under far better conditions than Mallie was suffering in Georgia. And so on May 21, 1920, Mallie Robinson took her five children (including sixteen-month-old Jackie) and set out for California. Together, they began a quest for a better life.

## Growing Up in Pasadena

Although they had a better life in Pasadena than in Georgia, Mallie and her children still struggled greatly in their new home. She worked as a maid for local white families and received government aid during times between jobs. Still, there were many days in which the family skipped meals, and some days in which there was no food at all.

Most days, Mallie got up before the sun and got home after dark, still managing to provide attention to her five children. She always emphasized the importance of family closeness, religion, and kindness to others. Eventually, her children went to work to help support the family. Jackie grew up in the Robinson home at 121 Pepper Street. His sister, Willa Mae, looked after him while Mallie was at work.

Willa Mae, who was three years older than Jackie, took him to school with her. Her teacher allowed him to play outside in the sandbox while his big sister sat in class near a window so that she could keep an eye on him. Young Jackie was happy enough with this arrangement, although he was pleased to graduate from the sandbox to the classroom when he became old enough to start his own education.

Pasadena, California, where Jackie grew up, has been the site of the famous New Year's Day Tournament of Roses parade since 1890. This photo is from the parade in 2004.

## First Encounters with Prejudice

Leaving Georgia and the Deep South did not mean leaving segregation and injustice behind. Pasadena had its own set of Jim Crow policies. Among other unfair practices, nonwhites were allowed to swim in the local Pasadena pool only one day per week. On this day, called International Day by the city, anyone could use the pool. This included the city's black, Japanese, Chinese, and Hispanic populations. At the end of International Day each week, the pool was drained and cleaned before the white people used it again.

When Jackie was eight years old, an incident took place that would help crystallize his anger toward injustice. He was sweeping the sidewalk in front of his house when a little white girl who was a neighbor started shouting at him, using the most offensive word she could think of to insult a black person. "Nigger! Nigger! Nigger!" she cried.

*When Jackie was eight years old, an incident took place that would help crystallize his anger toward injustice.*

Jackie shouted back, using the insult his brother told him was the worst thing you could call a white person. "Cracker! Cracker! Cracker!" he yelled. The little girl's father came out, and soon he and Jackie were throwing stones at each other until the man's wife came out and gave her husband a hard time for fighting with a child.

The Robinsons encountered many such incidents, including neighbors complaining that the children made too much noise or organizing petitions to get the Robinsons to move. Through this all, Jackie learned a very important lesson from his mother, which he would carry forward into his adult life.

Mallie never lost her temper at the white neighbors. She told her children not to go out of their way to antagonize people who disliked them, at the same time making it clear that she was not afraid of them, nor would she allow them to intimidate or mistreat her family. The Robinsons were there to stay.

## Early Athletic Ability

Jackie, whom some would come to call the finest all-around athlete the United States has ever produced, excelled in sports from an early age. Whether he was playing soccer, handball, or dodgeball in elementary school, Jackie mixed a desire to excel and win with his extraordinary physical gifts.

He was always the best player on the court, the team, or in the schoolyard. Led by Jackie, his third-grade soccer team beat the sixth-grade team. His sister, Willa Mae, recalled that "he was a special little boy, and ever since I can remember, he always had a ball in his hand."

His success in sports led Jackie's classmates of all races and social standing to like and accept him. He had white, black,

In California in 1925, Mallie Robinson poses with her five children for a family portrait. From left to right are Mack, Jackie, Edgar, Willa Mae, and Frank.

Mexican, Japanese, and Chinese friends with whom he played sports. They played with and against one another. In fact, the playing field of his elementary-school years was the one place where he was free from the racism that confronted him in all other aspects of his young life. This only cemented his belief that there was no place for racism in any sport, on any level, as well in the rest of life.

## The Pepper Street Gang

To earn money, Jackie cut lawns, had a paper route, and did errands for people in the community. But he also spent a lot of time with a group of friends who called themselves the Pepper Street Gang. This gang, made up of poor kids from his neighborhood, had black, white, Japanese, Chinese, and Mexican members.

Although they never committed violent crimes or intentionally hurt anybody, the members of the Pepper Street Gang did their share of mischief and had their run-ins with the law. They would throw rocks at passing cars, smash streetlights or windows, raid local fruit orchards, and shoplift food from stores.

Later in life, looking back at his youth, Jackie admitted that there was a chance he could have gone on to become a true troublemaker and never straighten out his life. Two factors prevented this from happening: one was sports, and the other was the influence of Reverend Karl Downs.

## Reverend Karl Downs

When Jackie was a young teen, a new minister arrived at his local church. Karl Downs had much in common with the teens he hoped to reach and help. He was in his twenties, not that much older than they were, and he was an athlete himself.

Recognizing that Jackie was a natural leader, Reverend Downs sought him out. In time, he convinced Jackie and his friends to join a young people's church program that included sports, dances, and other social events. The Pepper Street Gang even helped Reverend Downs build a youth center, which became a place where they could go and socialize or play sports rather than get into trouble on the streets. And Reverend Downs was always there to counsel Jackie in times of trouble.

Because he was spurred on by his own talent and drive, and by the encouragement of his family and Reverend Downs, sports continued to grow in importance in Jackie's life. Foreshadowing the multisport success that would catapult him to national notice a few years later in college, Jackie made the varsity team in football, basketball, baseball, and track at John Muir Technical High School.

> Because he was spurred on by his own talent and drive . . . sports continued to grow in importance in Jackie's life.

It was here, on organized school teams, that Jackie Robinson first felt the spotlight and enjoyed the success of being a star athlete. The fact that so much of his time was being taken up with practices and games left him little time to get into trouble with his Pepper Street buddies. He had taken a giant step away from the streets and onto the field of athletic competition, charting a course that would dominate the rest of his life.

# CHAPTER 2

# A College Star

*I was very much aware of the importance of being a team man [and] not jeopardizing my team's chances simply to get the spotlight.*

Already a local sports legend in Pasadena, in 1937 Jackie entered Pasadena Junior College (PJC). Here again, he not only played but also excelled in four sports: football, basketball, baseball, and track.

At PJC and everywhere else he ever played, Jackie's teammates spoke of how much he hated losing. While others would shrug off a bad game, he would brood about it, feeling he could have done better. His teammates also described him as an unselfish player. His burning desire to win was all about the team succeeding, not his individual glory. He pushed his teammates hard, but they respected him for his great sense of teamwork.

His influence and contribution were apparent, regardless of the sport. He led the PJC football team to an undefeated season, was the leading scorer on the basketball team, led

Jackie starred in four sports at Pasadena Junior College. Here, he poses with teammates on the baseball squad.

the baseball team to a championship, and set a record in the broad jump (now known as the long jump) as a member of the track team.

## Double Play

During his second year at PJC, Jackie took part in what has become a legendary moment in Pasadena history. The school had both a track meet and its championship baseball game scheduled for the same day in 1938. The two events took place forty miles apart, but there was no way Jackie could choose one event over the other. He felt that he owed it to himself and his teammates on both teams to be there for them.

He found a friend to drive him to the track meet, but because of a flat tire on the way, he was late and had no time to warm up. Rushing from the car right onto the field, he arrived just in time for the start of the broad jump. His jump of twenty-five feet, six inches that day set a new national junior college Amateur Athletic Union (AAU) record, breaking the previous mark held by his brother Mack.

Jumping back into his friend's car, Jackie changed into his baseball uniform as the car sped toward the baseball field forty miles away. Once again, dashing from the car and heading right onto the field, he arrived in time to play shortstop, get two hits, and steal a base, helping Pasadena win the championship.

## UCLA

Pasadena Junior College was a two-year school. So when the time came in 1939 for Jackie to leave PJC and continue his education elsewhere, many colleges offered him **scholarships**. His skills as an athlete meant that many schools offered him full tuition and living expenses.

# Mack Robinson

Jackie was not the only person in the Robinson family who would grow up to be a world-class athlete. His older brother Mack, whom Jackie idolized, was a member of the U.S. Olympic track team in 1936. The Olympics that year were held in Berlin, Germany. Adolf Hitler was already in power in Germany, although World War II had not yet begun. Hitler planned to use the Olympics as a way to show the world the superiority of Germans and of the white race in general. But an African American track star named Jesse Owens smashed those plans. He won four gold medals at the 1936 Olympics and emerged as the Games' biggest star. It is not as well remembered that Mack Robinson finished second to Owens in the two-hundred-meter dash to capture the silver medal.

Mack (far left) finishes second only to Jesse Owens (second from right) in the two-hundred-meter dash at the 1936 U.S. Olympic Team Trials in Randall's Island, New York. Mack later won a silver medal in the same event (again finishing behind only Owens) at the Olympics in Berlin that year.

After spending two years at Pasadena Junior College, Jackie attended the University of California at Los Angeles (UCLA). This photo is of Royce Hall, one of the four original buildings on the UCLA campus.

Of all these schools, Jackie was leaning toward the University of California at Los Angeles (UCLA). UCLA was known for its nationally ranked athletic teams. Also, Jackie had never lived far from home, and he didn't want to be far away from his family. UCLA was close enough that he could commute to school and still live at home. His brother Frank, one of Jackie's biggest fans and supporters, thought that UCLA would be a perfect choice. Jackie valued Frank's opinion greatly.

On May 10, 1939, while Jackie was still trying to make up his mind about where to continue his college education, word came that Frank had been killed in a motorcycle accident. Frank left behind a wife and two young children. Jackie, Mallie, and the rest of the family were devastated by this tragedy. Sadly and ironically, Frank's death helped Jackie make his decision. He would go to UCLA so that he could live at home and be near his mother and Frank's family. Shaken and shattered by the loss of his beloved brother, Jackie prepared for the next chapter of his own life.

He entered UCLA as a junior. There, Jackie once again achieved greatness in four sports. As a Bruin (the UCLA sports teams' nickname), under the national spotlight, Jackie took a giant leap from being a local California sports celebrity to becoming a nationally known athletic phenomenon. When athletes are selected for varsity teams, they are given cloth letters to sew onto their team jackets. This is known as lettering in a sport. Jackie became the first student-athlete at UCLA to letter in four sports: baseball, football, basketball, and track.

*. . . under the national spotlight, Jackie took a giant leap from being a local California sports celebrity to becoming a nationally known athletic phenomenon.*

Although Jackie and other African American student-athletes were welcomed to UCLA, in general the nonwhite student population was excluded from many of the school's social events. Though there were no specific rules against them attending, nonwhite students were expected not to show up at the school's parties and dances where students got to meet and mingle. As welcome as Jackie was made to feel on the playing field, he recognized the separate minority he belonged to as part of the overall student population.

## On the Field

Despite the social conditions at the school, UCLA had gained a reputation for giving African American athletes a chance to earn a place on school teams based on ability alone. Because of this, the school's teams had a large number of fans in black communities throughout the United States.

In no time, Jackie was dazzling football fans with his amazing running ability. Following a Bruin football game against the University of Washington, even the players on the University of Washington team admitted to the *Bruin* newspaper that "Robinson is the greatest thing we have ever seen. He twisted, squirmed, refused to be stopped."

When the football season ended, Jackie jumped right into basketball. He was a great passer and shooter, and his quickness once again served him well. He ended up leading the league in which UCLA played in scoring. Despite this statistic, Jackie was, above all, a team player.

Jackie poses for a basketball photograph at UCLA in 1940. He competed for the school in basketball, baseball, football, and track.

During his junior year, Jackie was competing for the national scoring title. His main rival was a player named Ralph Vaughn, who played for UCLA's biggest rival in all sports, the University of Southern California (USC). During a key UCLA game against Stanford University, the competition for the scoring title came to a surprising end.

The fans in the UCLA gym knew that Vaughn was also playing that night for USC in another game. With UCLA holding a narrow lead in its game against Stanford and time running out, Jackie chose to hold the ball, dribble, and pass rather than put up a shot and risk the other team taking possession of the ball and scoring. This was long before today's thirty-five-second clock used in men's college basketball, which limits the time each team has before they must put up a shot.

The crowd, aware that he was competing for the scoring title, kept screaming for Jackie to shoot to add to his personal point total. But he was more concerned with securing the victory. The better team strategy was to hold the ball and guarantee the team's victory. And that's what he did.

"Jackie thought of the score and the team," UCLA basketball coach Wilbur Johns said of his star player. "Nothing else counted. He always placed the welfare of his team above his chance for greater stardom."

## The Training Table

Just because Jackie had become a star college athlete didn't mean that his family had any more money at home. There were still many family members living under the same roof on Pepper Street, and food was still tight throughout Jackie's college career.

Because football and basketball were the most well-funded and high-profile college sports, UCLA provided a training table—a spread of food after a game or practice—for its players on these teams. They did this for the football and basketball teams, but not for track or baseball.

Partly because of this, football and basketball became Jackie's main focus. He knew he would be well fed during those seasons, which allowed his family to stretch what little food there was that much further.

Baseball season immediately followed basketball season. Playing baseball, Jackie did not put up the same kind of numbers he had in football and basketball. When baseball season ended, track season began, during which he won several broad-jump titles.

Although being a four-sport athlete brought him fame, Jackie later came to believe that all the physical stress his body went through playing sport after sport, throughout the year with no break, served to shorten his Major League Baseball career.

While at UCLA in 1940, Jackie competes in a track meet at the Los Angeles Memorial Coliseum. The Coliseum had been the site of the 1932 Olympic Games.

# Meeting Rachel

By the time his senior year at UCLA rolled around, Jackie was a national star. But as crucial as UCLA was for catapulting him to national sports prominence, perhaps the most significant thing that happened to him in his senior year was meeting a freshman who would, in time, become the most important person in his life.

"I didn't think anything could come into my life that was more vital to me than my sports career until Ray Bartlett, my best friend at UCLA, introduced me to Rachel Isum," Jackie later said of the woman who would become his wife, his greatest supporter, and his partner during the coming ordeals in breaking baseball's color barrier, the unwritten policy that kept black players out of the major leagues.

*Jackie had noticed the pretty freshman in the student lounge on campus but felt too shy to approach her.*

Jackie had noticed the pretty freshman in the student lounge on campus but felt too shy to approach her. When he mentioned how he felt to Bartlett, Jackie's friend set up the introduction. The two began dating, and Jackie soon discovered that not only was Rachel pretty, but also she was charming and very smart. She was a straight-A student studying nursing. Rachel, like everyone else on campus, knew who Jackie Robinson was. The handsome senior was a celebrity.

From a distance, Rachel thought Jackie was cocky and arrogant. She assumed that all his athletic success must have given him a big ego. In time, the soft-spoken young woman came to see the great intelligence and caring side of the superstar athlete.

# Rachel Isum

Rachel Annetta Isum was born in 1922 in Los Angeles. Her father, Charles Raymond Isum, worked for the *Los Angeles Times* for more than twenty years as a bookbinder. Her mother, Zellee Isum, ran her own catering business. Rachel learned about preparing food—and much more—from her mother. "She had impeccable manners; she was articulate, always proper, and she expected the same of me," Rachel said of her mother.

Rachel learned the value of work at an early age. When she was ten years old, she worked at the public library, where her mother sometimes provided food for events. Young Rachel earned fifty cents (six or seven dollars in today's money) for each event she worked.

After graduating from Manual Arts High School in Los Angeles, Rachel attended UCLA, where she met Jackie. Although best known as the woman who stood steadfastly beside Jackie Robinson, providing support and advice throughout his many trials in baseball and beyond, and who raised three children with him, Rachel forged a career for herself as well. She worked as a nurse, a professor of nursing at Yale School of Nursing, and a director of nursing at the Connecticut Mental Health Center. She is also the founder and a board member of the Jackie Robinson Foundation and one of the main keepers of her husband's **legacy**.

In 1940, when Rachel's father died, Jackie was there for her and her family. They clung together during this time of great sadness. Rachel's mother, Zellee Isum, who had liked Jackie from the start, appreciated the attention and support he gave to her family.

While at UCLA, Jackie met—and fell in love with—Rachel Isum. Their bond is evident in this photograph.

"In this time of sorrow, we found each other," Jackie later wrote. "I knew then that our relationship was to be one of the most important things in my life no matter what happened to me."

The two were soon deeply in love. But events both in their personal lives and in the world would shortly conspire to keep them from being together.

# CHAPTER 3

# In the Army

*I had no intention of being intimidated into moving to the back of the bus.*

During his senior year at UCLA, Jackie began thinking about his life after college. In early 1941, as he entered his final semester, Jackie felt a great responsibility to start making money as soon as possible to help his family.

In late February, when UCLA's basketball season ended, he decided to leave school, just a few months before he would have graduated. Those closest to him— his mother, Reverend Downs, and Rachel—strongly advised him to stay and get his degree.

But Jackie saw no advantage to having a college degree and also saw no future in pro sports for a black athlete. He was more interested in helping his mother by bringing money into the household right away. And so, despite the arguments by those he trusted most, Jackie left UCLA. He worked as an athletic director for a youth organization for a while. Then, in September of 1941, he took a job playing football for an integrated team called the Honolulu Bears, who were part of the semiprofessional Hawaii Senior Football League. Semipro athletes are paid for playing, but not enough to make a living. They must hold down other jobs.

Jackie played football on Sundays and did construction work during the week for a company located near Pearl Harbor in Hawaii. Football season ended on

After playing football at UCLA (above), Jackie continued playing the sport in a semipro league in Hawaii in 1941.

December 3. A few days later, Jackie was on a ship heading home to California when the news came that the Japanese had bombed Pearl Harbor. The United States had entered World War II.

## Lieutenant Jackie Robinson

Upon his return to Los Angeles, Jackie got a job working for Lockheed Aircraft. This was not a job he would have had a realistic chance of getting before the attack on Pearl Harbor. The aircraft industry generally did not hire black workers. But the urgent need for military equipment as the United States

# Attack on Pearl Harbor

On the morning of December 7, 1941, planes from the Japanese navy bombed the U.S. naval base in Pearl Harbor, Hawaii, in a surprise attack. The Japanese were upset with the United States because of President Roosevelt's ban on exporting products to Japan. Roosevelt put the ban into effect after Japan invaded China. World War II had been raging in Europe for two years already, but the United States had not yet gotten militarily involved. The attack on Pearl Harbor damaged U.S. battleships, destroyers, and aircraft. More than 2,400 people were killed, and more than 1,200 were wounded. The following day, the United States declared war on Japan and entered World War II. The leaders of Japan thought that the bombing would cause the United States to lift the ban. Instead, it "awakened a sleeping giant," according to Japan's Imperial Admiral Yamamoto, the man who planned and carried out the attack.

Jackie was en route to California from Hawaii on the day that the Japanese bombed Pearl Harbor in Hawaii (December 7, 1941). This famous photograph shows smoke billowing from the bombed USS *West Virginia* and USS *Tennessee*.

geared up for war opened doors that might otherwise have remained shut.

Also, throughout America, young men were registering for the draft, a system in which they were legally bound to serve in the military if called. "Being drafted was an immediate possibility, and like all men in those days I was willing to do my part," Jackie later wrote.

In March 1942, Jackie was drafted into the army and sent to Fort Riley in Kansas. He achieved much there and gained the respect of many, but he also faced racism and segregation in what he called the "Jim Crow Army." The U.S. armed forces were still segregated at that time. There were units made up of only white soldiers and others made up of only black soldiers, but blacks and whites did not serve or fight side by side in the same unit.

Jackie's college education gave him a leg up on many soldiers. He decided to apply to Officer Candidate School, which could make him a higher-ranking soldier in the army. He passed all the required tests, but along with all the other

Jackie is wearing his military uniform in this 1945 photograph. He served in the U.S. Army from March 1942 until his honorable discharge in November 1944.

## Segregation in the Military

African Americans have served in the U.S. military since the time of George Washington. More than five thousand black soldiers fought in the American Revolution. More than one hundred thousand black soldiers fought in the Civil War.

African American troops fought for the Union cause during the American Civil War, which lasted from 1861 to 1865. This 1865 photograph shows soldiers at Fort Corcoran in Arlington, Virginia.

When the United States entered World War II to fight for freedom in foreign countries, blacks in America were still being denied basic **civil rights** and freedoms. Still, more than two million black men registered for the draft and more than one million served in the armed forces during World War II.

But in all of these wars, black soldiers served in all-black units, separate from white soldiers. They had to use segregated toilets, drinking fountains, restaurants, and recreational facilities. Black soldiers fighting for freedom and equality overseas were being denied these things within their military units and back home in America as well.

Then, on July 26, 1948, President Harry S. Truman signed an executive order banning segregation in the military. It read: "There shall be equality of treatment and opportunity for all persons in the armed services without regard to race, color, religion, or national origin." Racial segregation in the military had finally ended.

This executive order of President Harry S. Truman, dated July 26, 1948, ended segregation in the U.S. military.

black applicants in his unit, he faced months of delays before he was finally accepted. After completing his officer training, he became a second lieutenant and volunteered to serve as the base's **morale** officer. But he still had to deal with the army's policy of segregated facilities for black and white soldiers.

As morale officer, he tried to arrange for more seating for black soldiers in the segregated base **canteen**, where the men under his command would go for snacks and relaxation. There were a limited number of seats assigned for blacks, who had to wait in line for these seats even when there were open seats in the white section.

Jackie made a phone call to a major on the base to explain the situation and request a change to the unfair policy. He was stunned and outraged by the response he got. "Well, let's be reasonable, Lieutenant Robinson," the major replied. "Let me put it to you this way. How would you like to have your wife sitting next to a nigger?"

After exploding on the phone, Jackie took his complaint about both the seating situation and the major's racism to his commander, who in turn brought it to a general. But nothing was ever done about either situation.

In another incident at Fort Riley, he went to try out for the camp's baseball team but was told he'd have play with the "colored team." He quickly discovered that there was no such team.

## Court-Martial

In 1944, Jackie was transferred to Fort Hood, Texas, where he took over as commander of the 761st Tank Battalion, an all-black unit. On the evening of July 6, Jackie boarded a shuttle bus used by members of the military. The bus company's

An American flag is unfurled at Fort Hood, Texas, in this undated photograph. Jackie was stationed at Fort Hood in 1944.

policy, which was tolerated by the U.S. Army, was that a limited number of African Americans were allowed on first so that they could take seats in the back of the bus. Then, even if additional black people had been waiting longer, the rest of bus was filled with whites.

While waiting for the bus, Jackie had run into the wife of one of his fellow officers. The two of them sat together in the middle of the bus. The woman, a light-skinned African American, was mistaken for a white woman. But the driver ordered Jackie to move to the back of the bus. He refused.

A confrontation with the bus driver led to the military police being called, and charges were pressed against Jackie. Most of them were made up, such as the charge that he was drunk. Jackie never touched alcohol throughout his life. The **court-martial** that was to come was obviously going to be a frame-up, built around false charges, but Jackie fought back.

He wrote a letter to the Secretary of War, knowing that the army would not want the bad publicity of an obviously racist and unjust trial. He also wrote to the National Association for the Advancement of Colored People (NAACP), the nation's premier civil-rights organization, knowing that word of a frame-up of a popular, prominent black athlete would spread. It did. Newspapers that were aimed at African American readers, known collectively as the black press, most notably the *Pittsburgh Courier*, picked up the story. The injustice Jackie faced became well known.

In addition, the officer assigned to defend Jackie made short work of the witnesses who were spewing rehearsed stories and memorized lies. The officer easily got these witnesses to contradict one another about what had happened on the bus, since none of them was actually telling the truth. Jackie was found not guilty and cleared of all charges. In November 1944, he was given an **honorable discharge**. His military career was over.

# CHAPTER 4

# A Fateful Meeting

*Mr. Rickey, are you looking for a Negro who is afraid to fight back?*

Before Jackie left the army, a fellow soldier who had played baseball with the Kansas City Monarchs of the Negro Leagues told Jackie that the Monarchs were looking for players. He suggested that Jackie write to the team. He did, and that letter started in motion events that would not only change his life and the game of baseball, but also would change America forever.

Jackie's first job after getting out of the army was teaching physical education and coaching the basketball team at Samuel Huston College in Austin, Texas, where his old friend Karl Downs was now president. Rachel remained in California to study nursing.

While working in Austin, Jackie heard back from the Kansas City Monarchs. They wanted him to try out for the team. If he proved good enough, he could have a job playing for them. In March 1945, Jackie left Samuel Huston College and joined the Monarchs for spring training.

## The Kansas City Monarchs

Jackie reported to the Monarchs, where he quickly made the team. But he began his first job as a professional baseball player with mixed feelings. He was glad for the opportunity to earn a living playing pro ball, an

Jackie wears his first professional baseball uniform in this 1945 photograph. He played for the Kansas City Monarchs of the Negro Leagues.

opportunity that was denied to African Americans by the major leagues. But his experiences in the army served only to strengthen his passionate opposition to Jim Crow segregation in any form. To Jackie, an all-black league was just another example of the Jim Crow policies he had battled in the army and when he was growing up.

He also wondered how this job could possibly help him down the road. There was no future in Major League Baseball for black players, so what was the point? While being paid to play baseball might seem like a glamorous idea, the reality of life in the Negro Leagues was very difficult. Travel schedules were grueling. The teams were poorly funded and managed. Many towns in which they played had no hotels for blacks—and those that did offered horrible accommodations. Finding a restaurant that would serve them also proved to be a challenge for Jackie and his teammates.

Still, from a baseball point of view, Jackie's time with the Monarchs was an important part of his education. Many great players filled the Negro Leagues. On the team bus to and from games, his Monarch teammates talked baseball all the time. They discussed fine points of strategy in all aspects of the game, from what a pitcher might throw to the best way to run the bases.

# The Negro Leagues

In 1884, two black players played in the major leagues. Then, at the end of that century, players (led by superstar Cap Anson), officials, and fans began a movement to ban black players.

In 1920, a former pitcher named Andrew "Rube" Foster organized a group of businessmen and sports reporters from the black press to set up a new league. The National Association of Colored Professional Base Ball Clubs was born. This league soon came to be called the Negro National League. In time, other all-black leagues were formed.

The Negro National League had eight teams, including the Kansas City Monarchs, for whom Jackie Robinson played in 1945. The league also featured some of the greatest baseball players ever to don a uniform, such as future Hall of Famers Josh Gibson, Satchel Paige, James "Cool Papa" Bell, William J. "Judy" Johnson, and Oscar Charleston. Rube Foster himself was inducted into the National Baseball Hall of Fame in 1981.

Other all-black leagues sprung up. The Negro Leagues, as the all-black leagues came to be called collectively, had their **heyday** from the early 1930s until the mid-1940s. Negro League baseball had become an important part of the segregated lives of black Americans. The Negro National League shut down in 1949, and the last Negro League, the Negro American League, disbanded in 1962.

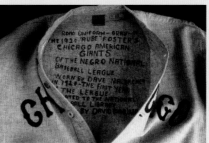

This Negro Leagues uniform was worn by "Gentleman" Dave Malarcher of the Chicago American Giants in 1920.

James "Cool Papa" Bell was one of the Negro Leagues' most exciting and respected players. Jackie learned a lot about baserunning from watching Cool Papa, who donated these items to the National Baseball Hall of Fame.

Jackie talked, but mostly he listened to guys who had been playing for years. And he learned.

"Tell him something once and you never had to tell him again," said Frank Duncan, Jr., a player with the Negro Leagues' Elite Giants and the son of the Monarchs' manager, Frank Duncan.

The player that Jackie learned the most from was James "Cool Papa" Bell. Bell was a legendary base stealer in the Negro Leagues. Jackie watched, learned, and imitated his moves. In time, **baserunning** and stealing bases would become Jackie's trademark in the major leagues.

As much as he learned from his fellow players, Jackie knew he was different from most of them. He was one of the few college-educated players in the league. He was soft-spoken and gentlemanly in a rough-and-tumble sport filled with players who drank, smoked, and partied to excess—all things the somber, serious Robinson did not do.

Perhaps the greatest strain on Jackie during his time with the Monarchs was his separation from Rachel. She was still back in California studying nursing while Jackie was traveling with the team. Jackie missed Rachel terribly and worried that their time apart might cause him to lose her. He wanted to marry her but not until he was sure about his future. But at that moment, his future, both personally and professionally, was very much up in the air.

## Clyde Sukeforth

On the baseball field, Jackie excelled as he had always done in every sport. Statistics from the Negro Leagues are not always reliable. But, to the best of our knowledge, in the 1945 season, his first in professional baseball, he led the Monarchs with a **batting average** well over .300, while playing in approximately forty-five league games.

Unknown to Jackie at that time was the fact that Branch Rickey, general manager of the Brooklyn Dodgers, had a plan to bring a black player to the major leagues. Not only did Rickey strongly believe in the integration of baseball, but he knew that the addition of talented black players would help his team win and help him make money.

Rickey sent his scouts, whose job was evaluating the ability of potential new players, to openly seek out top black players, telling everyone, including the scouts, that he was starting a new Negro League team. But this was not true.

When Jackie Robinson quickly moved to the top of Rickey's list based on his age and playing ability, Rickey looked into Jackie's background in California to find out what kind of man

# Branch Rickey

Branch Rickey was probably the most influential nonplayer in baseball in the twentieth century. As general manager of the St. Louis Cardinals in the 1920s, Rickey created the minor-league farm system still used by all teams today to scout and develop young players. He also set up the first full-time spring training facility, was the first to use batting cages and pitching machines to help players practice, and introduced the use of batting helmets for safety.

His greatest achievement, bringing Jackie Robinson to the majors, had its roots in his own experience. In the early 1900s, Rickey was the coach of the Ohio Wesleyan University baseball team. When his only black player, Charles Thomas, was refused a room in the hotel where the team was staying in South Bend, Indiana, Rickey protested strongly. He offered to have Thomas share his room, which the hotel finally allowed.

Rickey came into the room to find Thomas crying and trying to scratch the skin off his hands with his fingernails.

"It's my hands," Thomas cried. "They're black. If only they were white, I'd be as good as anybody then, wouldn't I, Mr. Rickey?"

"Charley," Rickey replied, "the day will come when they won't have to be white."

That scene haunted Branch Rickey for years, and decades later he did his part to help make his vow to Thomas come true.

he was. Rickey learned of Jackie's intelligence, strong character, commitment to family and faith, and avoidance of alcohol and tobacco. He also learned that Jackie had successfully played with and against white players in college.

He believed he had found the right man for the job. He knew that whomever he chose would be looked at closely by those who opposed integration, hoping to find fault not only with his playing ability, but also with his personal life and character.

In August 1945, Rickey sent one of his top scouts, Clyde Sukeforth, to Chicago, where the Monarchs were playing. Sukeforth was to watch Jackie play, then bring him back to Brooklyn, New York, for a meeting.

Jackie, meanwhile, had decided to give up baseball once the 1945 season with the Monarchs ended. He thought he would move back to California, look for a job as a high school coach, marry Rachel, and settle down. So when Sukeforth told him that Branch Rickey wanted to meet with him to discuss his playing for a new Negro League team, Jackie was less than enthusiastic. He was tired of the traveling, the poor conditions, and the separation from Rachel. He had had enough of all-black baseball.

Sukeforth then told Jackie that if he wouldn't go see Rickey, Rickey would come to see him. It was then that both men began to suspect that perhaps Rickey had something more in mind than a spot on a new Negro League team. They both knew that general managers almost never traveled to watch players. And this was even less likely to happen with Negro League teams. Jackie agreed to accompany Sukeforth back to Brooklyn.

## August 28, 1945

On the morning of August 28, 1945, Jackie Robinson and Clyde Sukeforth entered the darkly paneled office of Branch

Rickey on Montague Street in Brooklyn. Portraits hung on the wall, including one of President Abraham Lincoln, one of Rickey's heroes. Rickey, a large, imposing man with bushy eyebrows, glasses, and a deep booming voice, sat behind a big desk.

Rickey stared hard at Robinson. Jackie stared back. "He just stared and stared," Sukeforth later said, speaking of Branch Rickey. "Stared at him as if he were trying to get inside the man."

Rickey finally spoke, asking Jackie if he had a girl. Jackie thought this was

The Brooklyn Dodgers' Branch Rickey was a visionary executive who sought to end Major League Baseball's color barrier.

an odd question. And at that moment, given the fact that his relationship with Rachel was at a difficult point, he was unsure himself of the answer. Rickey then asked him if he knew why he had brought him there. Jackie repeated the story Sukeforth had told him about the new Negro League team.

That's when Ricky told him the truth. "I sent for you because I'm interested in you as a candidate for the Brooklyn National League Club," he said.

"I was thrilled, scared, and excited," Jackie later wrote of that moment. "I was incredulous." And for one of the few times in his life, Jackie Robinson was speechless. Rickey asked him if he thought he could do it. Jackie said yes.

Rickey explained that Jackie would start in Montreal, with the Dodgers' minor-league club, and if he succeeded there he would join the major-league Brooklyn Dodgers. Then Rickey, always known as a dramatic man, leaned across his desk, pointed a finger at Jackie, and barked, "I know you're a good ballplayer. What I don't know is whether you have the guts!"

Jackie was taken aback. Was this man questioning his courage?

Rickey went on to explain just how big the stakes were in breaking baseball's color barrier. If this move failed, it could be years or even decades before a black player would be considered again. He told Jackie how thoroughly he had searched for just the right man and how deeply he had investigated Jackie's life. He also explained that they would be on their own in what came to be called the Noble Experiment, and he talked about what tactics could and could not be used to accomplish this goal.

*Jackie was taken aback. Was this man questioning his courage?*

"We can't fight our way through this, Robinson," Rickey began. "We've got no army. There's virtually nobody on our side. No owners, no umpires, very few newspapermen. And I'm afraid that many fans will be hostile. We can win only if we can convince the world that I'm doing this because you're a great ballplayer and a fine gentleman."

Then, to illustrate his point, Rickey acted out all the horrible things he believed Jackie would face as the first black player in the majors: rude hotel clerks, waiters, and train conductors; opposing fans cursing at him and shouting horrible racial insults; opposing players throwing the ball at his head.

Then Rickey insisted that no matter what was said or done to Jackie, he could not fight back. He could not strike anyone or even lose his temper on the field.

When Rickey had finished with his performance, Jackie looked right at him and asked, "Mr. Rickey, are you looking for a Negro who is afraid to fight back?"

"Robinson!" Rickey boomed. "I'm looking for a ballplayer with guts enough *not* to fight back!"

It became clear to Jackie that he would have to hold his temper in the face of horrendous abuse. Rickey went on to explain that those who opposed integrating the national pastime would taunt and goad him, trying to provoke a fight that would frighten fans into not coming to games. This was how opponents

Branch Rickey and Jackie Robinson first shook hands to seal their historic agreement in 1945. This photograph was taken after the two men came to contract terms in 1948.

of integration hoped to prove that blacks should not be allowed into the majors. The only way for Jackie to defeat them, to prove them wrong, was to not fight back, to simply play ball as well as he could.

Jackie realized immediately that this would not be easy. He had always stood up for himself and fought back against injustice. But for this experiment to succeed, he realized that a new approach would be needed.

Rickey waited for Jackie's answer.

"I knew I had to do it for so many reasons," Jackie later wrote. "For black youth, for my mother, for Rae [Rachel], for myself. I had already begun to feel I had to do it for Branch Rickey."

Jackie agreed, and the two men shook hands.

Then Rickey asked Jackie to make several promises. He asked him to promise that he would hold his temper for three years no matter what happened. He also asked him to keep this news a secret from everyone except for Rachel and his mother.

Jackie agreed to these promises, then signed the historic agreement that would change baseball.

# CHAPTER 5

# The Montreal Royals

*It was probably the only day in history that a black man ran from a white mob with love instead of lynching on its mind.*

—Sam Maltin, writing in the Pittsburgh Courier,
*following the 1946 Little World Series*

For the next two months, Jackie told no one except Rachel and his mother about the deal he and Branch Rickey had made. The first thing he did when he returned home was to formally propose to Rachel. She accepted.

The wedding was set for the following February. Jackie would begin his first spring training in the Dodgers organization as a married man. He would have a steadfast, supportive partner by his side as he took on the greatest challenge of his young life. But first, the rest of the world had to learn about the momentous agreement he had signed in Brooklyn on that day back in August.

In 1945, Jackie proposed to Rachel, who helps him put on his coat in this undated photograph.

# The Bombshell Is Dropped

On October 23, 1945, Jackie went to Montreal to sign a contract with the Montreal Royals, a Dodgers minor-league team. He would play for the Royals in the 1946 season in preparation for the jump to the Brooklyn Dodgers the following year.

When word got out, reaction was immediate and varied. Reporters in the room were shocked as they hurried to phone the story into their newspapers back in New York. Branch Rickey, Jr., the Dodgers' farm director, was defiant, predicting that his father and the Dodgers "undoubtedly will be criticized in some sections of the United States where racial prejudice is rampant." Horace Stoneham, president of the Dodgers' biggest rivals, the New York Giants, supported the move, saying that it was "a fine way to start a program" and agreeing that Jackie was a good choice to begin the process of integrating baseball. Satchel Paige, the great Negro Leagues star, said, "They didn't make a mistake by signing Robinson. They couldn't have picked a better man."

Not everyone agreed. *New York Daily News* sports columnist Jimmy Powers predicted that Jackie would fail. Major-league pitcher Bob Feller, a future Hall of Famer, said that Jackie wouldn't make it in baseball because he was built like a football player, not a baseball player. "If he were a white man," Feller said, "I doubt they would even consider him as big-league material."

Branch Rickey defended his decision to the press by saying, "I have never meant to be a crusader. My purpose is to be fair to all people, and my selfish objective is to win baseball games."

On February 10, 1946, Jackie and Rachel were married by the Reverend Karl Downs. Having his longtime friend and **mentor** perform the ceremony meant a great deal to Jackie. Starting on the long, difficult road ahead with Rachel by his side meant everything to him.

# The Minor-League Farm System

Minor-league teams are professional baseball teams on which young players get their start and practice their skills. The best minor-league players eventually move up to join major-league teams.

Until the 1920s, almost all minor-league teams were independently owned. Then, while serving as the general manager of the St. Louis Cardinals in the 1920s, Branch Rickey came up with the idea of buying up a group of minor-league teams and making them all part of the Cardinals' organization. This system, which came to be called the farm system since it was where major-league talent was "grown," is still used by all major-league teams today. Teams now scout, sign, and develop young players, nicknamed "farm hands," on their minor-league teams in preparation for bringing the best players up to the majors.

Almost all major-league players begin their careers in the minor leagues, as Jackie did in 1946. This photograph is from a Brooklyn Cyclones minor-league game in 2007. (The Cyclones are a farm team for the New York Mets. Brooklyn has not had a major-league team since the Dodgers moved to Los Angeles in 1958.)

Jackie and Rachel were married at the Independent Church in Los Angeles on February 10, 1946.

In a couple of months, the baseball season would begin. The city of Montreal, a place not burdened with Jim Crow laws, was waiting to welcome Jackie Robinson warmly. But first came spring training, in the heart of the Jim Crow South.

## A Hard Time in Florida

A few weeks after their wedding, Jackie and Rachel were to fly to Daytona Beach, Florida, where the Royals held their spring-training camp. But things didn't quite turn out as planned. When the couple arrived for a connecting flight in the New Orleans airport, they were bumped to a later flight with no explanation. Then the airport coffee shop refused to serve them. Fortunately, Mallie had packed food for them, which they ate, stewing at this first of many injustices to come.

After waiting for twelve hours, they finally got on a plane. When the plane landed in Pensacola, Florida, for refueling, they were bumped off the flight again, their seats given to white passengers.

"I was ready to explode," Jackie later wrote. "But I knew that the result would mean newspaper headlines about an ugly racial incident and possible arrest not only for me but also for Rae."

Unable to find a hotel that would take them for the night, Jackie and Rachel boarded a bus for Jacksonville

Jackie boards a plane for one of his annual trips to spring training. His first spring training as a professional, minor-league baseball player was in Daytona Beach, Florida, in 1946.

and took seats that reclined, hoping to get some sleep. But the driver shooed them to the nonreclining seats in the back, where they sat upright for the sixteen-hour trip while the reclining seats, reserved for white passengers only, stayed empty.

The blacks-only section at the bus station in Jacksonville, where they waited for a bus for the final leg of the journey to Daytona Beach, was hot and filthy. They were running out of the food that Mallie had sent them off with and could find nothing to eat at the station. They were hungry, exhausted, and miserable when they finally reached their destination.

Rachel's first face-to-face encounter with the Jim Crow practices of the South left her more upset than she had ever been in her life. But it also "made me a stronger, more purposeful human being," she later said. "I think I was much more ready now to deal with the world we had entered." The couple stayed at the home of a local black political leader and community organizer, where, although they were made to feel welcome, they could not escape the fact that they were separated from Jackie's white teammates.

On the morning spring training began, Jackie faced the press for the first time as a member of the Montreal Royals. "Jack, do you think you can get along with these white boys?" one reporter asked.

"I've gotten along with white boys in high school, at Pasadena, at UCLA, and in the army," Jackie replied. "I don't see why these should be any different."

While at spring training in 1946, Jackie pauses outside the Dodgers' clubhouse door to wave to the cameraman. Until Jackie signed with the organization, the clubhouse was off-limits to African American ballplayers.

"What would you do if one of these pitchers threw at your head?" asked another reporter.

"I'd duck!" Jackie replied, cracking up the room.

Jackie's next obstacle was the Royals' manager, Clay Hopper. Hopper was a plantation owner in Mississippi who had begged Branch Rickey not to send Jackie to the Montreal club, claiming that he and his family would have to leave Mississippi if he was forced to have a black player on his team. Rickey, of course, ignored Hopper's request.

The spring-training games finally got under way, and Jackie saw what he would be up against on a regular basis when the Royals played throughout Florida. In Jacksonville, the team found the stadium padlocked because an integrated sporting event was a violation of local law. In Sanford, the game began and the crowd cheered for Jackie, but the police arrived and told Hopper he'd have to take Jackie out of the game because interracial athletic competition was against the law.

Branch Rickey, sitting with Hopper during one game when Jackie made a sparkling play in the field, called the move a superhuman play. Hopper, genuinely shocked, responded by asking, "Mr. Rickey, do you really think a nigger's a human being?" Rickey said nothing, not excusing what Hopper had said, but understanding how his background and upbringing would make him think that way.

But as Jackie's playing got better and better—soon he was hitting, fielding, and running as well as, if not better than, any other player on the team—Hopper came to begrudgingly accept him. Rickey knew that at each step on his journey, Jackie's ability on the field would be the best antidote to prejudice.

# Welcome to Montreal

As the regular season began, a local sportswriter in Montreal wrote, "For Jackie Robinson and the city of Montreal, it was love at first sight." Jackie and Rachel rented an apartment in the French-Canadian section of town. Neighbors were kind to the couple, and kids would follow them down the street hoping for a glimpse of this player who was quickly becoming a local hero. Canada, it seemed, had a very different attitude toward black people than the United States did. To add to their happiness, Rachel told Jackie that she was pregnant.

This is an aerial view of Roosevelt Stadium in New Jersey in the 1940s. Jackie made his debut for the Montreal Royals against the hometown Jersey City Giants at this site in 1946.

In the season opener, played in Jersey City, New Jersey, Jackie had an astounding debut, announcing with his bat, glove, legs, and baseball mind that he was capable of playing ball with anyone. He had four hits, including a home run. He also stole two bases, leading his team to a 14–1 victory. And he served notice to the baseball establishment that a new kind of player, with a new style of play, had entered the game.

Whenever he reached third base, Jackie would dance off the base as the next batter came up, break toward home plate, then dart back to third. Pitchers were so rattled by this behavior, which was extremely uncommon at that time in baseball, except for the Negro Leagues where Jackie had learned it, that they would have trouble concentrating on pitching to the next batter.

As the season progressed, Jackie came to realize that he was becoming more than just a baseball player and in some ways more than just a man. He was at the heart of a great social experiment whose success or failure would affect so many more people than just himself. He was becoming a symbol of great change while being asked to put up with insult, injury, even the threat of death, without being allowed to complain and without much help. Jackie knew very well that the Noble Experiment had no chance of succeeding unless, under all this pressure, he could play baseball at the highest possible level.

*As the season progressed, Jackie came to realize that he was becoming more than just a baseball player and in some ways more than just a man.*

That is exactly what he did. He finished the 1946 regular season in Montreal leading the International League (the minor league in which Montreal played) in hitting, with a .349 batting average, also a Royals team record, and in runs scored (113). He also finished with the highest **fielding percentage** in the league. He was voted the league's Most Valuable Player, leading the Royals to the most wins in their history (100) and attracting the largest crowds, both home and away, they had ever drawn.

## The Little World Series

In the 1946 Little World Series, the championship series of the minor leagues, the Royals played the Louisville Colonels. The first three games were in Louisville, Kentucky, where Jackie experienced the most vicious racial hatred and nonstop booing he had yet encountered anywhere.

Shaken, Jackie got just one hit in the first three games, and the Royals lost two of the three. They would now have to win three of the remaining four games to win the series.

But when the series moved to Montreal, things were very different. The Montreal fans, knowing what Jackie had endured in Louisville, turned their anger vocally on the entire Louisville team, booing every single Louisville player nonstop from the moment he stepped from the **dugout** to the time he returned.

Jackie had never heard his hometown fans give anyone this kind of treatment, but he was grateful for their support. "When fans go to bat for you like that, you feel it would be easy to play for them forever," he said after the series.

Inspired by their fans, the Royals swept the next three games at home to win the series. Jackie, after his rough start, ended up batting .400 for the series. He scored the winning run in the last game.

After the game, when Jackie stepped out onto the street, he was stunned to be greeted by a huge mob of fans who were waiting to thank him and bid him good-bye. Although no official

Jackie is pictured in a pregame pose in a Montreal Royals uniform in 1946. He helped the team win the Little World Series that season.

announcement had been made yet, these loyal fans were certain that next season their hero would be playing in Brooklyn in the major leagues.

They grabbed him, hugged him, and slapped his back. Kids grinned and women kissed him. "It was probably the only day in history that a black man ran from a white mob with love instead of **lynching** on its mind," Sam Maltin wrote in the *Pittsburgh Courier*, describing the scene.

But the moment that stood out most for Jackie had taken place a short while earlier, while he was still celebrating with his teammates in the Montreal clubhouse. Royals manager Clay Hopper, cleaning out his locker to head home to his Mississippi plantation, came up to Jackie and extended his hand. "You're a great ballplayer and a fine gentleman," Hopper said. "It's been wonderful having you on the team."

# The First Season

*The Brooklyn Dodgers today purchased the contract of Jackie Roosevelt Robinson from the Montreal Royals. He will report immediately.*

> —Branch Rickey, in a Brooklyn Dodgers press release, April 10, 1947

On November 18, 1946, Jackie Robinson, Jr., was born. While Jackie and Rachel enjoyed their first few months as new parents, an unspoken question lingered not only in their minds, but also in the minds of all baseball fans, New Yorkers, and many others around the country. Where would Jackie Robinson be playing when the following spring arrived?

In December, the only person who knew the answer to that question, Branch Rickey, attended baseball's winter meetings,

Jackie Robinson, Jr., was born in November 1946. Young Jackie poses with Mom and Dad in this photo in their New York home early in 1947.

an annual gathering of all the team owners and top executives of Major League Baseball. A vote was taken on whether baseball should be integrated, and fifteen of the sixteen teams voted against integration. Rickey and the Dodgers were the only team to vote in favor of it. Seeing this, Rickey realized that he had to take his next steps slowly and cautiously.

He moved the location of spring training in 1947 for both the Dodgers and the Royals from Florida, where Jackie had faced so much abuse, to Cuba and Panama, where Rickey hoped that race would not be such an issue. But even in Cuba, Jackie couldn't escape unfair Jim Crow rules. The white players stayed in a luxury hotel in Havana, while Jackie and the three other black players in spring-training camp stayed in a dingy downtown hotel. Jackie was furious at the unequal treatment,

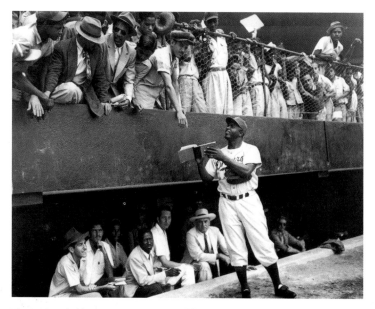

The Dodgers held spring training in Cuba and Panama in 1947. In this photo, Jackie signs autographs for fans in Havana, Cuba.

but Rickey explained to him that the white locals and the white American tourists at the luxury hotel—most of whom insisted their hotel be segregated—would complain. "I can't afford to take a chance and have a single incident," Rickey explained to Jackie. "This training session must be perfectly smooth." Jackie understood Rickey's reasoning, though it didn't make him feel any better about the unequal treatment.

## The "Revolt"

Rickey also faced another problem much closer to home. Word got back to him that some of his own Dodgers players, those born in the South, were putting together a petition stating that if Robinson made the Brooklyn team, they would not play with him. Rickey enlisted the help of Leo "The Lip" Durocher, the Dodgers' fiery, hot-tempered manager. Durocher didn't really feel strongly either way about Rickey's plan to integrate the game. He simply knew, as his players would come to discover in time, that a player with Jackie's talent would make them all winners and thus enable them to earn more money. After gathering his players together, he spoke in his own unique manner.

"I don't care if the guy is yellow or black or if he has stripes like a zebra!" Durocher blustered. "I'm the manager of this team,

Jackie talks things over with Dodgers manager Leo Durocher in this photo from 1948. Durocher saw beyond the color of Jackie's skin and recognized his immense baseball talent.

and I say he plays. What's more, I say he can make us all rich. And if any of you can't use the money, I'll see that you're traded!"

Rickey then called the four ringleaders into his office individually and blasted them, telling each one that anyone who was not willing to have a black teammate could quit. The revolt ended before it began.

## Brooklyn at Last

During the previous season, Jackie had played second base for the Royals. In 1945 he had also played some shortstop for the Monarchs. But the Dodgers had two well-established, well-liked players at those positions—Pee Wee Reese at shortstop and Eddie Stanky at second base—and Jackie had made it clear the previous year in Montreal that he was not out to take anyone's job away. What the Dodgers needed badly was a first baseman. So, although he had never played the position, Jackie took a first baseman's mitt and spent the spring learning to play first base.

On April 9, the Dodgers were shocked when manager Leo Durocher was suspended for the entire season by the baseball commissioner. Durocher was accused of associating with gamblers, but Rickey believed that the charge was made up by

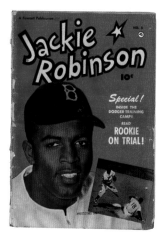

Jackie became so widely known that he was even featured in this comic book.

Yankees owner Larry MacPhail, a strong opponent of integrating the game. MacPhail hoped that getting rid of Durocher would prevent Rickey from bringing Robinson to the majors that year. He could not have been more wrong.

On the very next day, April 10, 1947, during the sixth inning of an exhibition game between the Royals and Dodgers at Ebbets Field, the Dodgers' home ballpark in Brooklyn, a press release was tacked to the bulletin board in the stadium's press box. It read simply: "The Brooklyn Dodgers today purchased the contract of Jackie Roosevelt Robinson from the Montreal Royals. He will report immediately." It was signed by Branch Rickey.

Jackie Robinson had been promoted to the Brooklyn Dodgers. What many suspected was now officially confirmed. In five days, Jackie Robinson would open the 1947 baseball season as a member of the Brooklyn Dodgers, becoming the first African American to play in the major leagues since Moses Fleetwood Walker in 1884. Telephone and telegraph wires in the press box blazed with the news, and reporters clacked away on their typewriters hurrying to break the momentous story.

On April 14, Rachel and Jackie Jr. flew in from Los Angeles. Jackie met them at the airport and accompanied them to their new living quarters at the McAlpin Hotel in Manhattan. Early the next morning, Jackie set out for Ebbets Field to play his first game as a Brooklyn Dodger. Rachel, along with Jackie Jr., who was then five months old, would be in

Before making his major-league debut in 1947, Jackie shook hands with Brooklyn Borough President John Cashmore. Standing next to Cashmore is former U.S. Senator James Mead (D-New York).

# The Brooklyn Dodgers

There may never have been a more beloved baseball team than the Brooklyn Dodgers. They began as part of a league called the American Association, where they played from 1884 to 1889. From 1890 until their devastating departure from Brooklyn in 1957, "Dem Bums," as they were affectionately called by their fans, were sometimes one of the best teams in the National League. Unfortunately for their fans, almost every time they made it to the World Series (except for 1955), they were beaten by their crosstown rivals from the American League, the New York Yankees. The Brooklyn fans' motto became "Wait 'til next year!" This reflected both the frustration of losing to the Yankees year after year and the eternal optimism and hope that sustained their fans through the long, cold, baseball-less winters.

The heyday of the Brooklyn Dodgers was the 1940s and '50s, when they earned the title "the Boys of Summer," capturing the hearts of working-class Brooklynites who identified with the players. Many of them, including Jackie Robinson, were their neighbors. The Dodgers finally won their only World Series in Brooklyn in 1955, beating the Yankees. However, after the 1957 season, owner Walter O'Malley moved the team to Los Angeles, where they still play, making him one of the most despised men in the history of Brooklyn and breaking the hearts of millions of loyal fans.

Shown above is a vintage Brooklyn Dodgers team pennant. The team played in the New York City borough from the inception of the franchise in 1884 (when the team was known as the Brooklyn Atlantics) through 1957.

The *Pittsburgh Courier* heralded Jackie's first big-league game with this edition. Although he did not get a hit, he reached base on an error and scored the winning run.

the stands later that day to witness the historic event and root on her husband and his new team.

Jackie Robinson's major-league debut was less than spectacular. In his first game, he did not get a hit, but got to base on an **error**. Things didn't get much better over the next few games as Jackie found himself mired in a deep batting slump, getting very few hits. His manager, Burt Shotton, who had replaced Leo Durocher, was a quiet, patient man, in many ways Durocher's opposite. Shotton supported and encouraged Jackie and, most importantly, kept him in the lineup. Luckily, the removal of the combative Durocher in favor of Shotton left Jackie with a manager more suited to his personality and to the difficult task at hand.

## Insults, Threats, and Abuse

During the early part of the season, Jackie's biggest problems were his lack of hitting and the cancellation of games on the road due to poor weather. Left with time to kill in unfamiliar, sometimes hostile cities, Jackie couldn't join his teammates as they went to eat in segregated restaurants. He hadn't yet made friends with anyone on the team, so on days he couldn't go the ballpark, he was left alone and isolated in his hotel room. *New York Post* sportswriter Jimmy Cannon, who covered the Dodgers, called him "the loneliest man I have ever seen in sports."

What surprised Jackie the most was the lack of the racial abuse he had experienced in the minors. His opponents so far had shown great restraint, even as Jackie braced himself for the insults and attempts to injure him that Branch Rickey had acted out that day in his office. But all that came to an end when the Dodgers came home to Ebbets Field on April 22 to play the Philadelphia Phillies.

Phillies manager Ben Chapman, who had been born in Alabama, poured foul-mouthed insults and racial slurs from the Philadelphia dugout starting right in the first inning. His players joined in the chorus of hatred and what Branch Rickey would later call "unconscionable abuse."

From the moment Jackie strode to the plate in the first inning, he was stunned by the viciousness he was hearing—not in the Deep South, as had been the case with the Royals, but here, in his home ballpark in Brooklyn. Horrible references to slavery and personal insults to Jackie and his family came hurling toward him.

Jackie felt tortured. He tried his best to ignore all this and just play ball, but he seethed inside, and his performance on the field suffered. For a moment, he considered throwing it all away, rushing into the Phillies dugout and smashing in the teeth of Chapman and his players.

Then he remembered the promise he had made to Branch Rickey. He remembered the responsibility he felt to black athletes and all black people across America. He knew he had to make Rickey's Noble Experiment a success for so many more people than just himself.

As the game progressed, help came from the only place it could—Jackie's Dodgers teammates. Chapman's torrent of hate infuriated them. They all knew of Jackie's promise to not fight back, and they banded together as a team to support and defend him. Eddie Stanky shouted at the Phillies, "Listen, you yellow-bellied cowards! Why don't you pick on somebody who can answer back?"

The press picked up on the story and jumped all over Chapman. Branch Rickey later drew the ironic conclusion that "Chapman did more than anybody to unite the Dodgers. He solidified and unified thirty men, not one of whom was willing to sit by and see someone kick around a man who had

Jackie's Dodgers teammates stood up for him during his rookie season in 1947. Here, he poses on opening day with (from left to right) Spider Jorgensen, Pee Wee Reese, and Eddie Stanky.

his hands tied behind his back. Chapman made Jackie a real member of the Dodgers."

The support of his Dodgers teammates, however, did not stop the problems with other teams. The St. Louis Cardinals planned a player strike when the Dodgers came to town. A local sportswriter exposed the plot, and National League President Ford Frick notified the Cardinals that any player who participated in the strike would be suspended from the league. "The National League will go down the line with Robinson whatever the consequences," Frick announced.

"This is the United States of America, and one citizen has as much right to play as another."

> *"This is the United States of America, and one citizen has as much right to play as another."*

When the Chicago Cubs voted to strike, word got out, and the league office sent a telegram saying that anyone who didn't play would be barred from baseball for life. But that didn't stop the Cubs' pitchers from throwing at Jackie's head each time he came to bat. This was especially dangerous, as batters did not yet wear the plastic helmets they wear today.

The most serious offenses came in the form of hate mail pouring into the Dodgers' offices. Death threats came in, as well as threats to kidnap Jackie's wife and son. In Cincinnati, threats from the Ku Klux Klan, a violent, racist organization, prompted the FBI to search the roof of the ballpark and nearby buildings for snipers.

In one game, the Cardinals' Enos Slaughter hit a ground ball and ran to first base where Jackie was playing. Instead of going for the base as Jackie took the throw, Slaughter aimed the sharp cleats on the bottom of his shoes right at Jackie, slashing his leg.

On the road, while his teammates stayed in fancy hotels, Jackie would often stay at the home of a local black family or in a hotel for blacks only. He ate his meals alone. The camaraderie of teammates, which broke up the loneliness of the road for other players, eluded him. All of this got to Jackie, who slept fitfully and felt constantly anxious.

## Hitting His Stride

Several turning points took place early in the season. Pee Wee Reese, the popular Dodgers shortstop, was a southerner from Kentucky. Those who opposed Jackie's entrance to the big leagues tried to stir up

Jackie poses before a game in his rookie season in 1947. He batted .297 that year while stealing twenty-nine bases and earning Rookie of the Year honors.

rumors that Reese resented this black man, whom they claimed was trying to take away his job. But Reese supported Jackie from the start: "When I first met Robinson in spring training, I figured, well, let me give this guy a chance. It may be he's just as good as I am. Frankly, I don't think I'd stand up under the kind of thing he's been subjected to as well as he has."

As it turned out, Reese's actions spoke more loudly than his words. During a game in Boston, the Braves' players heckled Jackie mercilessly. Then they turned their venom on Reese, getting on him for being a southerner who agreed to play with a black man. Reese walked over to first base from his position at shortstop, put his hand on Jackie's shoulder, and began talking, as ballplayers often did. This symbolic gesture quieted the taunts and marked the start of a close friendship between the two men that would last for the rest of Jackie's life.

In a game against the Pittsburgh Pirates, Jackie reached first base, where he stood beside Pirates first baseman Hank Greenberg. Greenberg, one of baseball's few Jewish players, was in the final year of a Hall of Fame career as one of the game's greatest home-run hitters. He had suffered **anti-Semitic** abuse from players and fans throughout his career and could understand some of what Jackie was going through.

"Stick in there," Greenberg said as Jackie stood beside him at first base. "You're doing fine. Keep your chin up." Jackie greatly appreciated the support.

Crowds began turning out in record numbers to see Jackie play, both at home and on the road. And black fans started flocking to the ballpark like never before, a fact that was not lost on the baseball team owners. They saw the effect that having black players on their teams could have on their profits. More fans meant more money for the owners.

One Sunday afternoon at Ebbets Field, as the Dodgers were warming up for a game against the Giants, the crowd began buzzing at the arrival of Joe Louis, the heavyweight boxing champion and perhaps the most popular black athlete in America at that time. Jackie trotted over to where Louis was sitting and shook his hand. The huge crowd at Ebbets Field roared its approval. "This was a turning point," said Dodgers broadcaster Red Barber. The

Ebbets Field was the famed ballpark of the Dodgers from 1913 to 1957. In this photo, Jackie heads home after a game during his rookie season.

# Red Barber

Though he started as a radio announcer in 1934 with the Cincinnati Reds, Red Barber will always be identified with New York City baseball. In 1939, he became the voice of the Brooklyn Dodgers, where he remained until 1953, when he moved across town to become the Yankees' announcer.

Barber worked both on radio and television. He broadcast the first baseball game ever televised in 1939. Known for his accuracy in describing the action, he never rooted for the home team on the air, as some other announcers did. He always presented a fair view of the game.

Barber was also known for his colorful catchphrases such as "Oh, Doctor!" (for a great play) and "What a rhubarb!" (for a fight on the field). His eye for detail and his smooth, impartial style helped him become one of the most influential announcers in sports history.

When Jackie Robinson joined the Dodgers, Red Barber didn't know what to make of this revolutionary event. Barber, born in Mississippi and raised in Florida, was unsure about the Noble Experiment. He expressed his concerns to Branch Rickey. Rickey explained to Barber that his opinions didn't matter. He was hired to tell listeners what was happening on the field, and that was his one and only concern. Barber understood and went on to become one of Jackie Robinson's biggest supporters.

Former Dodgers radio announcer Red Barber is pictured here in 1949. A native of the South, Barber took some time to warm to the presence of an African American in the majors, but he eventually became one of Jackie's biggest fans.

Brooklyn community, black and white, had fallen in love with Jackie Robinson.

As April gave way to May, Jackie got hot. He got one or more hits in fourteen straight games, batting .395 during that stretch. He tore up the base paths, stealing bases (including home), rattling opposing pitchers with his speed and energy, and bringing the Negro Leagues' energetic style of play to the major leagues.

At that point, his teammates, opposing players, fans around the country, and the press took notice of what Branch Rickey knew all along—that is, just how great a player Jackie Robinson could be. "He became the biggest attraction in baseball since Babe Ruth," Red Barber reported. Branch Rickey told some of his friends, "You haven't seen Robinson in action yet—not really. You might not have seen him at his best this year at all, or even next year. He's still in his shell."

## Speed in Baseball

Why was Jackie's speed such a big part of his success? In baseball, when a player hits the ball and reaches base safely, he becomes a base runner. His job then becomes to get around the bases and back to home plate as quickly as possible. Sometimes this is with help from his fellow batters, who try to hit the ball so that the runner can advance to the next base. Being able to run between bases very fast makes the runner better able to advance without getting tagged out. If the batters do not hit, however, the runner can "steal" the base by running just as the pitcher throws to the plate. While many players had used speed as a baseball weapon before, Jackie's skill, speed, and daring let him bring that offensive play to a whole new level.

Jackie finished his first season batting .297 and winning the first ever Rookie of the Year award, given to the top first-year player in the major leagues. The Dodgers won the National League pennant, or championship, finishing with the best record in the league, and although they lost to the Yankees in the 1947 World Series, in every way Jackie Robinson's first year in the majors was a success. He had proven himself to be a true baseball talent, shattering the myth that black players weren't good enough to compete against

Jackie had a good season under difficult circumstances in 1947—but it was only the beginning of a Hall of Fame career.

white players and becoming a national hero in the process for his courage in the face of horrendous abuse.

On the home front, the Robinson family moved out of the hotel in which they had been living and into an apartment in Brooklyn. Jackie's first season had been a triumph. But the best was yet to come.

# CHAPTER 7

# Most Valuable Player

*I have no intention of creating problems. I am just
no longer going to turn my cheek to insults.*

The year 1948 began on a sad note for the Robinsons.
In February, as Jackie was getting ready to head to the
Caribbean to start spring training for his second big-league
season, he received the tragic news that the Reverend
Karl Downs had died in Texas at the age of thirty-five
from complications following stomach surgery. Jackie was
devastated. Downs had been a friend, mentor, and spiritual
leader for Jackie since his teenage years. He would be
sorely missed. Jackie traveled to Texas for the funeral,
then on to spring training with a heavy heart.

Jackie's baseball
season got off to a rough
start as well. He arrived
at spring-training camp
that year twenty-five
pounds overweight.
Following the 1947

After an off-season on the
banquet circuit, Jackie was
noticeably heavier entering
the 1948 season. He shed the
extra weight and had a good
year, although not one up to
his standards.

season, he had become a national star and a hero in black communities all across America. He did commercials, theatrical performances, and speaking tours. He was the guest of honor at many dinners, including those held by the NAACP, the civil-rights organization that would come to play such a huge role in his post-baseball life. As Jackie and Rachel toured the country, they were treated to tremendous hospitality and fine home-cooked meals—lots of them. "We ate like pigs, and for me it was disastrous," Jackie later wrote.

Leo Durocher was back as the Dodgers' manager after having been suspended for the entire 1947 season. The outspoken and abrasive Durocher rode Jackie hard about his weight, pushing him to get into shape in a hurry. Working hard under the hot Caribbean sun, Jackie dropped most of his extra weight.

During the off-season, Jackie, Rachel, and Jackie Jr. had moved from their apartment into a house they rented in a different Brooklyn neighborhood. When word got out that a black family was going to move into the white neighborhood, some neighbors tried to organize a petition to prevent it. But most of their new neighbors refused to sign the petition, and the Robinsons were soon welcomed. They formed lifelong friendships with some of their white neighbors.

Back on the field, Jackie had another good year. He finished the 1948 season batting .296, leading the Dodgers in runs scored, and leading all National League second basemen in fielding percentage. Jackie had moved to second base that year, his more natural position, and formed one of the all-time great **double-play** combinations with shortstop Pee Wee Reese. He also got a black teammate when future Hall of Fame catcher Roy Campanella joined the Dodgers. But the Dodgers had an off year, finishing in third place.

# NAACP

The National Association for the Advancement of Colored People (NAACP) is the nation's oldest civil-rights organization. Founded in 1909 by journalist William English Walling and social workers Dr. Henry Moscowitz and Mary White Ovington, the NAACP works for fairness and equality for all people. It works with governments to change laws that discriminate and to pass laws that guarantee human rights. Some of its achievements include helping to bring an end to segregation on transportation in the South, the Civil Rights Act of 1964, and the Voting Rights Act of 1965. Some of its more famous members include Thurgood Marshall and Rosa Parks.

This poster is from an NAACP membership drive in 1949.

In July, with the season well under way, blustery Leo Durocher left the Dodgers to become manager of the rival New York Giants. Soft-spoken Burt Shotton, who had been such a big help to Jackie during his rookie year, returned as manager. When the 1948 season ended, despite what most would consider a good year, Jackie was disappointed in his own performance. "I was miserable," he later said,

This is Jackie's second baseman's glove, which is housed at the National Baseball Hall of Fame. After playing exclusively at first base as a rookie in 1947, he played more games at second base than at any other position during the rest of his career.

"because I knew that I should have done better—much better. I made a solemn vow to redeem myself and the Dodgers in 1949."

## MVP

In the off-season, Jackie did not repeat the mistakes he had made the year before. He watched what he ate and stayed in shape by playing on a barnstorming team, along with Dodgers teammate Roy Campanella. Barnstorming teams are teams that travel around the country and to other countries to play exhibition games against local teams. These are games that are not part of any official league schedule. Sometimes, the barnstorming teams are already existing teams. Other times, they are "pick-up" teams, brought together just for the tour.

Shortly before the 1949 season began, Branch Rickey called Jackie into his office. When Jackie had signed their agreement back in 1945 to play for Rickey starting in '46, he had also agreed to hold his temper and not fight back for three years.

Those years were now up. Rickey, who appreciated how fervently Jackie had held up his end of that agreement, let him know that starting with the 1949 season, he was free to be himself.

Rickey knew of the tension and nervousness his restraint had caused Jackie. He believed that having those limitations removed—making Robinson no different than other ballplayers, who were all free to fight back against dirty plays, scream at umpires, and stand up for themselves—would free Jackie, allowing him to improve his performance on the field. Rickey, once again, was right.

Shown here is the front of a baseball card from Jackie's career. He played ten seasons in the big leagues, all of them for the Brooklyn Dodgers, from 1947 through 1956.

"I have no intention of creating problems," Jackie told baseball commissioner Happy Chandler following his meeting with Rickey. "I am just no longer going to turn my cheek to insults."

Freed from these constraints, Jackie had the best season of his career. He led the league in batting (with a .342 average) and in stolen bases (with 37). He was given the National League's Most Valuable Player (MVP) award. This award is given every year to the player in each league who has done the most to help his team win. Not only did Jackie put up tremendous personal numbers, but also he led the Dodgers to another pennant, although they lost once again to the Yankees in the World Series.

Jackie did stand up for himself during his MVP season. But some sportswriters reacted poorly to this new behavior. If a group of Dodgers spoke up about a bad call or unfair play, it was Jackie who would be singled out as being a hothead. "As long as I appeared to ignore insult and injury, I was a **martyred** hero," Jackie said of this change in attitude by the sportswriters. "But the minute I began to answer, to argue, to protest, I became a swellhead, a wise guy, an upstart, a troublemaker, a sorehead."

He felt that if a white player argued, it was reported in the newspapers that he was simply showing spirit. But when Jackie did the same thing, he was accused of being ungrateful for the opportunity he had been given to play in the major leagues. He was pleased to not have to hold his tongue anymore, but very disappointed in the negative reaction he received for once again simply asking to be treated like everyone else.

This photograph shows Jackie attempting his signature play: a steal of home. He stole home 19 times in his career, which remains the most of any player in the post–World War II era.

# New Arrivals, Honors, and Responsibilities

The year 1950 got off to a joyous start for the Robinson family with the birth of their second child, Sharon, in January. The previous year, the Robinsons had moved from Brooklyn and finally bought a home of their own, in the St. Albans neighborhood of Queens, New York, so there was more room for the growing family.

More honors and awards were heaped upon Jackie as his fame continued to grow. He started doing two weekly sports shows on TV, plus a daily radio show in which he talked about almost anything, from the world of sports to community and political events. A movie about his life, which would star Jackie as himself, was also in the works. He now wanted to use his fame as a force for good, on both a personal and a political level.

He worked with children, coaching them and helping them improve their sports skills, at the YMCA in Harlem, a black

A movie still from *The Jackie Robinson Story* is shown here. Jackie played himself in the 1950 motion picture.

neighborhood in New York City. He would remain connected to the Harlem YMCA for the rest of his life. He also made many unpublicized visits to sick children in hospitals.

Politically, he became interested in the Anti-Defamation League (ADL), a group founded to battle anti-Semitism. He met with Arnold Forster, the ADL's leader, and tried to learn and use some of the group's techniques for fighting injustice and discrimination in his lifelong quest for equality for African Americans.

During that off-season, Jackie also went on a barnstorming tour with his Dodgers teammates Roy Campanella and pitcher

## Anti-Defamation League (ADL)

The Anti-Defamation League was founded in 1913 by a Chicago lawyer named Sigmund Livingston "to stop the **defamation** of the Jewish people and to secure justice and fair treatment to all." The organization, which still exists today, fights anti-Semitism and all forms of **bigotry**. Its goals are justice and equal treatment for all citizens and stopping discrimination against individuals or groups. The ADL uses education and media programs to spread its views. It also works with governments around the world to pass laws that ensure fairness while also fighting to end hate crimes. It fought to remove hateful stereotypes from newspapers, and by 1920, most of these had disappeared. In the 1920s, the ADL battled the Ku Klux Klan by exposing its members and their violent actions to the general public. In the 1930s the group monitored and exposed Nazi operators in the United States. In the years since, they have worked hard to expose bigotry wherever it is found.

Don Newcombe, the third black player to join the Dodgers and the 1949 Rookie of the Year. Larry Doby, the first African American to play in the American League, was also on that team.

## End of an Era

The Dodgers were favored to win the pennant by most sportswriters and fans in 1950, but the season ended in bitter disappointment when the Philadelphia Phillies won instead, clinching the pennant on the very last day of the season. Jackie had another great year, hitting .328, though not up to the level of his MVP season.

Even more crushing to Jackie than not winning the pennant was the announcement made after the 1950 season that Branch Rickey would be leaving the Dodgers to become the general manager of the Pittsburgh Pirates. Walter O'Malley took over the team following a power struggle with Rickey. O'Malley's political

Branch Rickey (left) and Walter O'Malley (center) chat with National League President Ford Frick in 1951. This was the year after Rickey left the Dodgers and O'Malley took control of the team.

and financial maneuverings left Rickey with no choice but to sell his interest in the team.

O'Malley didn't like Rickey. And he didn't like Jackie Robinson, especially the "new" Jackie Robinson, who was outspoken and demanded equal treatment. "O'Malley's attitude toward me was viciously [hostile]," Jackie later wrote. The two butted heads for Jackie's remaining years with the Dodgers. In time, O'Malley would come to be hated throughout Brooklyn when he moved the team to Los Angeles.

*In time, O'Malley would come to be hated throughout Brooklyn when he moved the team to Los Angeles.*

Rickey's achievements with the Dodgers were many. None were more important or more well known than his having had the courage and wisdom to break baseball's color barrier precisely when he did and with precisely the right man for the job. Still reeling from Rickey's departure, Jackie wrote to him, "It has been the finest experience I have had being associated with you, and I want to thank you very much for all you have meant not only to me and my family but the entire country and particularly the members of our race." Jackie said more than once that in many ways, Branch Rickey became the father he never really had.

Rickey's grandson, Branch B. Rickey, put it this way: "Sometimes my family believed that my grandfather really had two sons—my father [Branch Rickey, Jr.] and Jackie. We knew that my grandfather loved Jackie, and we all respected Jackie."

Of Robinson, Branch Rickey later said, "There was never a man in the game who could put mind and muscle together quicker and with better judgment than Jackie."

The two remained close friends for the rest of their lives.

# CHAPTER 8

# Champions at Last

*"Wait 'til next year!"*

> —*A cry uttered by fans of the Brooklyn Dodgers as they suffered repeated World Series losses to the New York Yankees*

Once again, in 1950, Jackie kept busy in the off-season. He continued his work with the Harlem YMCA, visiting schools across the city to encourage young people to stay in school and avoid getting into trouble with the law as he had done as a youth. He raised funds and collected toys to give out to poor children at Christmas. He also went on a barnstorming tour and did his best to keep in shape.

The Brooklyn Dodgers were once again the favorites to win the National League pennant in 1951. They pulled away to a big lead as the season began. In mid-August, though, the rival New York Giants began storming back. Eventually, New York caught Brooklyn. The two teams finished the

Jackie often could be found at the Harlem YMCA, as he is in this photo, counseling youngsters about sports and about life.

regular season in a tie for first place, forcing a three-game playoff that the Giants won on Bobby Thomson's home run, called the Shot Heard 'Round the World, in Game Three.

The Giants took the National League pennant, keeping the Dodgers out of the World Series for the second year in a row. Jackie, disappointed as all the Dodgers were, had one of his best all-around seasons in the majors (a .338 average, 19 home runs, and 88 **RBI**), but his teammate Roy Campanella won the MVP award.

Campanella was one of many successful African American players in baseball, thanks to Jackie Robinson, Branch Rickey, and their Noble Experiment. By the end of 1951, a mere four years after Jackie broke the color line, there were fourteen black players in Major League Baseball, including five All-Stars, and thirteen of the sixteen major-league teams had at least one black player in the minors.

## A New Home and Business

In 1952, Jackie had another good year. This time, the Dodgers won the pennant, but lost once again to the Yankees in the World Series. That year also brought the birth of Jackie and Rachel's third child, David. Following the 1952 season, Jackie branched out in his

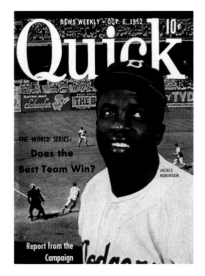

Jackie was on this magazine cover around World Series time in 1952. He had another all-star season that year as the Dodgers won the first of back-to-back National League pennants.

# The Shot Heard 'Round the World

Because the Dodgers and Giants finished in a tie for first place in 1951, a best-two-out-of-three playoff series was held to decide who would win the National League pennant and go on to the World Series. The Giants won the first game, and the Dodgers won the second. The third game, which would decide the pennant, was played on October 3 at the Polo Grounds, the Giants' home stadium, in New York.

In the ninth inning of Game Three, the Dodgers led 4–2. Brooklyn fans throughout the borough huddled close to their radios, fingers crossed, poised to celebrate. But the Giants had two runners on base. The Dodgers brought Ralph Branca in to pitch to the next batter, Bobby Thomson. Thomson slammed Branca's second pitch into the left-field stands for a three-run, game-winning, pennant-clinching home run. The Giants fans sat in stunned silence for a moment. Then they erupted. Final score: Giants 5, Dodgers 4.

Russ Hodges, the Giants' radio announcer, delivered one of the most famous play-by-play calls of all time. He screamed over and over, "The Giants win the pennant! The Giants win the pennant! The Giants win the pennant!" Thomson's home run came to be known as "The Shot Heard 'Round the World."

And heartbroken Brooklyn Dodgers fans would once again have to wait until next year.

It was the "Shot Heard 'Round the World." Giants slugger Bobby Thomson is mobbed at home plate after hitting the home run that gave his team the National League pennant in a playoff with the Dodgers in 1951. Jackie (42) watches the scene as losing pitcher Ralph Branca (far right) begins the long walk to the clubhouse beyond center field.

The Dodgers celebrate a victory over the New York Yankees at Ebbets Field in Game Three of the 1953 World Series. The Yankees went on to win the Series in six games, however, marking the second year in a row that they foiled Brooklyn's championship hopes.

non-baseball activities. In addition to his radio and television shows and his community and charity work, he opened a men's clothing store in Harlem. Jackie had another great season in 1953, and the Dodgers won the pennant by a wide margin. But again, in a scenario that was by now all too familiar to Brooklyn fans, the Dodgers lost to the Yankees in the World Series.

In 1954, Rachel began house hunting for a new, bigger home for their growing family. But in many of the places she looked, in New York and Connecticut, she encountered racism in the real-estate market. When she offered to pay the full price that one house was selling for, the owner immediately pulled it off the market. The owners of another house that was up for sale refused to even show it to Rachel.

A series of articles about antiblack practices in Connecticut housing appeared in a local newspaper and prompted a meeting of concerned citizens. Among those attending the meeting was Andrea Simon, the wife of a major book publisher. Rachel and Andrea hit it off and began what would become a lifelong friendship. With Andrea, a prominent white woman in the community, lending a hand, Rachel soon found a piece of property in Stamford, Connecticut, that seemed perfect for the new Robinson home. Their new house was built on the property, and the family moved in the following year.

The 1954 season was a disappointment for the Dodgers. They finished second behind the Giants. Jackie had a good year statistically but a rough year in other aspects of the game. During a rainy game in Milwaukee, Jackie got ejected for giving an umpire a hard time. When he flipped a wet, slippery bat toward the dugout, it accidentally flew into the stands. Although this was clearly an accident (even the umpire he was arguing with said so), and the bat didn't actually hit anyone, fans began booing him. As word of this incident spread, relentless booing followed him wherever he played. Adding to his troubles was a new manager, Walter Alston, who was not friendly toward Jackie and refused to back him up in arguments.

Through the years of the 1950s, with his restraints removed, Jackie fought back and spoke out freely against bad calls or mistreatment of any of his teammates. He viewed these actions as simply being a good teammate and doing what many other players did. But he was accused by the press of being a loudmouth, being a crybaby, or getting a swelled head. And for the first time he heard boos, not because he was a black player in a white man's game, but from fans who preferred the quiet Jackie who took it all and never retaliated. But that man was never who he really was, and he had decided that he would never again hold back his true beliefs or his strong emotions about what happened on or off a baseball field.

## Next Year Is Finally Here

The year 1955 started out with the Robinson family moving into their new house in Connecticut. The year also began with rumors that Jackie might be washed up, be traded to Pittsburgh to be reunited with Branch Rickey, or simply retire from the game he had given so much to. None of those was true.

Although injuries to his knee and ankle kept him from playing in a third of the Dodgers' games that season, and he ended the year with the lowest batting average of his career (.256), the season proved to be a magical one for the team. Brooklyn won the pennant and, once again, in what had become an almost annual tradition, faced the Yankees in the World Series.

Despite Jackie's steal of home in Game One of the series, the Dodgers lost at Yankee Stadium, where they also lost Game Two. Heading back to Ebbets Field, down two games to none, the Dodgers' faithful fans prepared themselves for yet another disappointing World Series outcome. But Brooklyn won all three

The 1955 season was a very good one for Jackie and the Dodgers. Here, he celebrates a victory with teammates Clem Labine (left) and Carl Erskine (right).

games at home and headed back to Yankee Stadium with a 3–2 lead in games, needing just one more win in the best-4-out-of-7 series to claim the championship.

The Yankees won Game Six at Yankee Stadium, tying the series at three games apiece. Once again, it would all come down to Game Seven. This time, behind the strong pitching of Johnny Podres and a game-saving catch by outfielder Sandy Amoros, the Dodgers won the game 2–0. The "next year" for which their fans had been waiting for so long had finally come to Brooklyn. The Dodgers had won the World Series for the first time in their history, and for what would turn out to be their only time in Brooklyn.

Jackie celebrated with his teammates and with the rest of Brooklyn. He was praised in newspapers as the heart, soul, and inspiration of the team that finally beat the Yankees.

Brooklyn players rush the pitcher's mound to celebrate after the final out of the 1955 World Series. The Dodgers overcame the rival Yankees in seven games in the Series to win their lone championship while based in Brooklyn.

# CHAPTER 9

# Endings and Beginnings

*The way I figured it, I was even with baseball and baseball with me. The game had done much for me, and I had done much for it.*

No one, not even Jackie himself, knew if he would be back with the Dodgers in 1956. His disappointing performance in 1955, his nagging knee and ankle injuries, and the tense relationship he had with Dodgers owner Walter O'Malley all contributed to the uncertainty. "It's up to the club," Jackie said at the time. "I'm going to do what they want. I want to play for them."

During the off-season, as Jackie thought about his future and what lay ahead for him in a world that might no longer include baseball, on December 1, 1955, a black woman named Rosa Parks refused to give up her seat on a Montgomery, Alabama, bus to a white passenger. Her action ignited a bus boycott, during which black people in Montgomery stopped using the buses. This protest against Jim Crow laws quickly became a nationally recognized event in the growing civil-rights movement. The boycott was led by Dr. Martin Luther King, Jr. "The more I read about the Montgomery situation," Jackie said at the time, "the more respect I have for the job [the civil-rights leaders] are doing."

The year 1955 was a pivotal year in the civil-rights movement. Efforts in the South to prevent blacks from

# Rosa Parks and the Montgomery Bus Boycott

Rosa Parks, the woman whose brave action sparked what would come to be called the beginning of the modern civil-rights movement, was born in 1913 in Alabama, where bigotry and violence were everyday occurrences. "I remember going to sleep as a girl hearing the [Ku Klux] Klan ride at night and hearing a lynching and being afraid the house would burn down," she later said in an interview.

On December 1, 1955, she got on a public bus to go home from her job as a seamstress in a department store. When the bus got crowded, the driver told Mrs. Parks to give up her seat so that a white person could sit. She refused.

The bus driver told her she was breaking the law—segregation was legal in Montgomery at that time—and that he would call the police. She still refused to move, and she was arrested.

This incident led to the formation of the Montgomery Improvement Association, led by Dr. Martin Luther King, Jr. This group organized a boycott of the city-owned bus company. Most of the forty thousand black commuters in Montgomery used carpools, cabs, or walked instead of taking the bus. The boycott lasted for 382 days and led to a U.S. Supreme Court decision that outlawed racial segregation on public transportation. Rosa Parks became a national hero among those who believed in equality.

This is the Montgomery, Alabama, bus on which Rosa Parks refused to give up her seat to a white passenger in 1955. The bus is on display at the Henry Ford Museum in Dearborn, Michigan.

voting were increasing. The number of lynchings increased as well. A black fourteen-year-old named Emmett Till, who was visiting Mississippi from Chicago, was murdered. Schools in the South fought the growing effort to end segregation. The NAACP was at the forefront, battling against these injustices. Jackie became more and more interested in the organization and how he might help them even as he pondered the 1956 baseball season and his life after the game.

Dr. Martin Luther King, Jr., became the most influential leader in the civil-rights movement. This photograph is from August 28, 1963, the day that King delivered his famous "I have a dream" speech in Washington, D.C.

## The Final Season

Jackie did play for the Dodgers in 1956. But in his tenth season of Major League Baseball, he still faced bigotry and Jim Crow rules. In Alabama, fans still shouted racial insults from the stands. In Miami, the black players on the Dodgers still had to stay in an inferior hotel separate from the white players.

A rising, growing, national civil-rights movement was taking

Though 1956 brought the end of Jackie Robinson's pro baseball career, fans can still enjoy viewing his equipment, such as this bat, which is on display at the National Baseball Hall of Fame.

up the cause, organizing and formalizing the battle against injustice and inequality, a battle Jackie had been fighting his entire life, often by himself. He now sought ways to lend his fame, reputation, voice, and passion to that movement even as the clock on his baseball career began to tick down.

Both Jackie and the Dodgers had strong seasons in 1956. The Dodgers won the pennant on the last day of the season and again met the Yankees in the World Series, which the Yankees won. All in all, during Jackie's ten big-league seasons with the Dodgers, he helped lead the team to the World Series six times. Each of those times they played the Yankees. And, except in 1955, they lost each of those series.

This baseball card is from late in Jackie's career. In his final two seasons, 1955 and 1956, he mostly played third base for the Dodgers.

## The Next Chapter Begins

Jackie believed he could come back for one more season in 1957, despite the constant pain he had to endure. His knees and ankles ached all the time. His body was starting to break down, a process that would continue, increasing in speed and intensity, for the rest of his life. The pace at which he had pushed his body—starting back in college, playing four sports without a break, followed by twelve seasons of professional baseball—was taking its toll. Also, the effect on his body of the stress of being baseball's racial pioneer while having to keep his reaction to abuse and injustice inside should not be underestimated.

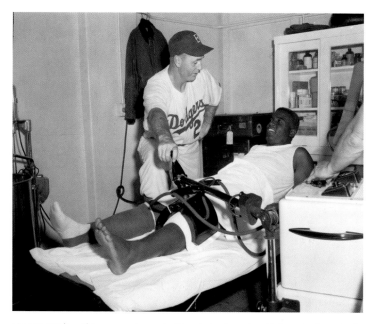

Manager Walter Alston supervises as Jackie gets treatment on his knee in the trainer's room in 1955. Jackie's many years of athletics took a toll on his body.

In addition to the physical pain he was suffering, Jackie grew tired of spending so much time away from his family, a necessary but difficult reality of life as a baseball player. Since 1955, when he began to seriously consider retirement from baseball, he had been looking for business opportunities for his post-athletic career. He knew he would be involved with the civil-rights movement as much as he could, but he also needed to make a living.

This was many years before baseball players signed the multimillion-dollar contracts of today, and so even the highest-paid players of Jackie's time, of which he was not one, needed to think about earning a living once they hung up their uniforms. Jackie thought about staying in the game as a coach or manager, but realized that although black players were now common in the majors, the barrier to teams hiring black coaches and managers had yet to be broken. He preferred to channel his efforts fighting injustice into other avenues. And no one offered him the opportunity to stay in baseball after his playing days ended, anyway.

This is Jackie's Brooklyn Dodgers cap from the National Baseball Hall of Fame. Jackie never played for any other team in the majors.

December 1956 was one of the most eventful months in Jackie's life. On December 1, he got a phone call from William Black, the president of Chock Full o' Nuts, a chain of inexpensive restaurants in New York City. The two met for lunch, and Black offered Jackie a job as vice president and director of personnel. A civil-rights supporter, Black, a white executive, hired a large number of African American employees when many others did not. Jackie said he would consider the offer and reply soon.

After careful consideration, Jackie decided to accept William Black's offer, retire from the Dodgers, and begin his life after baseball. But there was a complication.

Two years earlier, he had signed an agreement with *Look* magazine giving it the exclusive rights to the story of his retirement, whenever it occurred. This meant that the magazine, and nobody else, got to break the story to the public. Because of this, even after he signed a deal with Chock Full o' Nuts, Jackie would have to remain silent about the fact that he had chosen to end his baseball career.

One more complication popped up. Jackie had scheduled a meeting with William Black for December 12 to sign his employment contract with Chock Full o' Nuts. On December 11,

# William Black

William Black started out selling nuts on the streets of New York City in 1922. His business did so well that a few years later he opened a series of small stores, which all sold a variety of nuts. In 1931, when the Great Depression was underway, nuts became something of a luxury item, so Black changed some of his nut stores into restaurants where he sold inexpensive sandwiches and coffee. The Chock Full o' Nuts restaurants caught on, and by the 1950s, they had spread throughout the city.

Right from the start, Black was known as a generous employer. He gave out Christmas bonuses each year and provided health insurance and retirement plans for his employees at no cost to them. He was also known for hiring both blacks and whites to work in his restaurants, which was not a common practice in the 1950s.

Chock Full o' Nuts founder William Black (pictured here) offered Jackie a rewarding post-baseball job.

he got a phone call from the Dodgers telling him that general manager Buzzie Bavasi wanted to meet with him the next day. Jackie explained that he couldn't make it but that he would try to call Bavasi.

The following day, Jackie signed his Chock Full o' Nuts contract, then called Bavasi,

*. . . Jackie decided to accept William Black's offer, . . . and begin his life after baseball.*

only to be informed that the Dodgers had traded him to their crosstown rivals, the New York Giants. When news of the trade got out, Dodgers fans became incensed that the team would trade their hero to the "enemy." Bavasi explained the trade by saying that he needed to make room for a younger player, and he knew that Jackie would not want to leave New York.

Jackie told the Giants that if he decided to play next year at all, he would be happy to play for them. But the trade confirmed the decision he had already made. When the *Look* magazine story finally broke, the world knew that Jackie Robinson's baseball career was over.

"The way I figured it," Jackie said when he was finally free to speak about his retirement, "I was even with baseball and baseball with me. The game had done much for me, and I had done much for it."

The Dodgers accused Jackie of deception in pretending that he would accept the trade. He told the Giants that his decision to leave baseball to pursue other business opportunities had nothing to do with the trade. In a return letter, Giants president Horace Stoneham, an early supporter of Branch Rickey's decision to bring Jackie to the majors, wished him success and wrote, "I can't help thinking it would have been fun to have had you on our side for a year or two."

# CHAPTER 10

# Life After Baseball

*Baseball was just a part of my life. Thank God that I didn't allow a sport or a business or any part of my life to dominate me completely. I felt I had my time in athletics, and that was it.*

In March 1957, as the Dodgers prepared for their first season in ten years without Jackie Robinson, and for what would turn out to be their final season in Brooklyn, Jackie began his job at Chock Full o' Nuts. Like many others in business, he commuted from his home in Stamford, Connecticut, to New York City.

Jackie's new career gave him much more time to enjoy at home with his family. Nothing gave him or them more pleasure. That same year, he also began work as the chairman of the NAACP's Freedom Fund Drive. The organization's many civil-rights activities cost money, and this annual fund-raising drive was a key way in which they got the funds they needed. William Black, Jackie's new employer, had made it clear when he hired him that Jackie was free to take time off from his job for outside activities.

As a well-liked and popular figure, Jackie was a perfect choice for this position. But he didn't want to just be a famous face and name who posed for pictures and signed letters, while others did all the hard work. As with everything he did in his life that was important to him, he wanted to throw himself fully into this effort and be

After retiring from baseball, Jackie was involved in several causes. In this photo from 1959, he sits next to Eleanor Roosevelt (third from left) while waiting to speak at the Manhattan School for Boys. Roosevelt, wife of former president Franklin Delano Roosevelt, was herself an outspoken human rights activist.

a team player. So Roy Wilkins, the executive secretary of the NAACP, sent Jackie on a fund-raising tour in which he could visit many of the organization's 1,500 branches around the country.

A young NAACP lawyer named Frank Williams was enlisted to travel with Jackie and help him prepare for the many fund-raising events he would be attending. Williams filled him in on the history of the NAACP and the many cases the organization had won in courts all around the country, including the Supreme Court. As Williams, a long-time Robinson fan, later recalled, he was very nervous about how to "prepare this famous baseball star to become a civil-rights spokesman." But in the end, he did just that.

Working together, they made an exciting and effective fund-raising team. Jackie gained confidence and experience that he would apply to all his future civil-rights activities.

# Richard Nixon

Fund-raising and court cases were an important part of the work of the NAACP and the civil-rights movement in general, but Jackie knew that to make significant, permanent changes, the political system would have to be used. He believed that civil-rights legislation was necessary. In a speech during the NAACP fund-raising tour, he called for laws that "ensured that Negro citizens shall be protected in exercising the rights and privileges guaranteed by the Constitution."

In violent response to the successful bus boycott in Montgomery, black churches were bombed. Jackie called on President Eisenhower to take action, stating, "I have the greatest

Chock full o'Nuts

425 LEXINGTON AVENUE
New York 17, N. Y.

May 13, 1958

The President
The White House
Washington, D. C.

My dear Mr. President:

I was sitting in the audience at the Summit Meeting of Negro Leaders yesterday when you said we must have patience. On hearing you say this, I felt like standing up and saying, "Oh no! Not again."

I respectfully remind you sir, that we have been the most patient of all people. When you said we must have self-respect, I wondered how we could have self-respect and remain patient considering the treatment accorded us through the years.

17 million Negroes cannot do as you suggest and wait for the hearts of men to change. We want to enjoy now the rights that we feel we are entitled to as Americans. This we cannot do unless we pursue aggressively goals which all other Americans achieved over 150 years ago.

As the chief executive of our nation, I respectfully suggest that you unwittingly crush the spirit of freedom in Negroes by constantly urging forbearance and give hope to those pro-segregation leaders like Governor Faubus who would take from us even those freedoms we now enjoy. Your own experience with Governor Faubus is proof enough that forbearance and not eventual integration is the goal the pro-segregation leaders seek.

In my view, an unequivocal statement backed up by action such as you demonstrated you could take last fall in deal-

The President        Page 2        May 13, 1958

ing with Governor Faubus if it became necessary, would let it be known that America is determined to provide -- in the near future -- for Negroes -- the freedoms we are en-titled to under the constitution.

Respectfully yours,

Jackie Robinson

JR:cc

In 1958, Jackie wrote this letter to President Dwight D. Eisenhower, urging action on civil rights.

respect for President Eisenhower, but he must step into the breach in this situation and show that the U.S. government will not condone these bombings. Our struggle for civil rights is the struggle of all Americans."

By 1960, Jackie had gotten skillful at juggling his role in the business world and as a civil-rights leader. In addition, while continuing the radio program he had been doing for ten years, he began writing a regular column in the *New York Post*, an influential and widely read daily newspaper.

In his column, he wrote about sports, national politics, international affairs, and, of course, civil rights. People were listening to him, and politicians knew that his opinions and endorsement carried a lot of weight and, they hoped, a lot of votes as well.

In the 1960 presidential race, Jackie gave his support to Republican Richard Nixon. This was a decision he would later regret. His sole interest in backing a presidential candidate was to support the person whom he felt would do the most good in bringing equality and an end to injustice for black Americans.

Nixon spoke often in the 1950s and during the 1960 presidential campaign about the need for civil rights. The Democratic candidate, Senator John F. Kennedy, had a poor voting record in the Senate when it came to civil rights. Jackie felt that as president, Nixon would do more good for black Americans than Kennedy would. Jackie also did not want to link himself to one party only. African Americans at the time were commonly drawn to the Democratic party, but Jackie felt that it was important to draw black voters into both political parties.

Jackie hoped that Nixon would keep his promises to fight for civil rights. Kennedy won and became president in 1960. True to Jackie's concerns, Kennedy did very little during his

Jackie poses with presidential candidate Richard Nixon on the campaign trail in 1960. Nixon lost the 1960 election to John F. Kennedy.

presidency to advance the cause of civil rights. When Nixon eventually became president in 1968, Jackie was very disappointed in his civil-rights policies as well.

The years following 1960 were increasingly busy ones in the civil-rights movement. Lunch-counter demonstrations and **sit-ins** increased, and Jackie continued to work hard for the cause in which he so believed. But his relationship with the NAACP became strained. Roy Wilkins resented Jackie's support of Nixon, whom he saw as doing too little for civil rights, and also of Dr. King, whom he viewed as too radical in his approach to change.

## The Hall of Fame

In January of 1962, Jackie was given baseball's highest honor. He was elected to the National Baseball Hall of Fame, becoming the first black player to be immortalized alongside the game's other all-time greats. After sharing the news with his immediate family, he quickly made two phone calls: one to his mother, the other to Branch Rickey.

"I feel so strongly and deeply about being a member of the Hall of Fame," Jackie wrote in his newspaper column, which was then being published by the *Amsterdam News*, "that I almost am at a loss to explain those feelings to readers. If this can happen to a guy whose parents were virtually slaves, a guy from a broken home, someone who in his early years was a delinquent—then it can happen to you."

# National Baseball Hall of Fame

The National Baseball Hall of Fame & Museum is located in a small rural town in upstate New York called Cooperstown. It is visited by thousands of people each year who flock to the tiny village of fewer than three thousand residents to learn about baseball's history, look at objects from its storied past, and celebrate the game's greatest players.

The museum was started by Cooperstown businessmen Stephen C. Clark and Alexander Cleland in 1934. Contributions and priceless baseball memorabilia came pouring in from all over the country as word of the museum spread. When Clark told National League President Ford Frick about the museum, Frick suggested coupling the museum with a Hall of Fame to honor the great players, managers, umpires, and executives of the sport. Clark agreed.

In 1936, the first five players were chosen for induction by the Baseball Writers' Association of America. They were Ty Cobb, Babe Ruth, Honus Wagner, Christy Mathewson, and Walter Johnson. In 1939, the museum opened its doors to the public. In the years since, hundreds of additional baseball greats have been inducted into its hallowed halls.

The exterior of the National Baseball Hall of Fame & Museum is shown here. The building opened in 1939.

A few days before Jackie's induction into the Hall of Fame, a dinner was held in his honor at New York's Waldorf-Astoria Hotel. New York Governor Nelson Rockefeller, who attended, called Jackie "a hero of the struggle to make American democracy a genuine reality for every American." In addition to those in attendance, messages of congratulation were sent from many people.

Richard Nixon and President Kennedy both sent messages. A message from Dr. King explained why he felt a man some saw as just a former athlete had every right to be the civil-rights spokesman he had become: "He has the right because back in the days when integration wasn't fashionable, he underwent the trauma and the humiliation and the loneliness which comes with being a pilgrim walking the lonesome byways toward the high road of freedom. He was a sit-inner before sit-ins, a **freedom rider** before freedom rides. And that is why we honor him tonight."

Three days later, on July 23, 1962, in the beautiful rural hamlet of Cooperstown, New York, Jackie Robinson was officially welcomed into the National Baseball Hall of Fame. During his induction address, he told the adoring crowd that he would not have been there that day without the advice and guidance of three people, who, thankfully, were all there. He then called

JACK ROOSEVELT ROBINSON
"JACKIE"
BROOKLYN, N.L., 1947-1956

A PLAYER OF EXTRAORDINARY ABILITY RENOWNED FOR HIS ELECTRIFYING STYLE OF PLAY. OVER 10 SEASONS HIT .311, SCORED MORE THAN 100 RUNS SIX TIMES. NAMED TO SIX ALL-STAR TEAMS AND LED BROOKLYN TO SIX PENNANTS AND ITS ONLY WORLD SERIES TITLE, IN 1955. THE 1947 ROOKIE OF THE YEAR, AND THE 1949 N.L. MVP WHEN HE HIT A LEAGUE-BEST .342 WITH 37 STEALS. LED SECOND BASEMEN IN DOUBLE PLAYS FOUR TIMES AND STOLE HOME 19 TIMES. DISPLAYED TREMENDOUS COURAGE AND POISE IN 1947 WHEN HE INTEGRATED THE MODERN MAJOR LEAGUES IN THE FACE OF INTENSE ADVERSITY.

This is Jackie's current plaque at the National Baseball Hall of Fame. His original plaque in 1962 featured his baseball accomplishments. The current plaque, which was unveiled in 2008, also includes his legacy as a civil-rights pioneer.

Branch Rickey, his mother, Mallie, and his wife, Rachel, to stand by his side. "Today," he said, "it seems that everything is complete."

## Trouble in Harlem

Throughout 1962, Jackie's time and energy were being stretched thin. Between his job at Chock Full o' Nuts, his work in the ongoing civil-rights struggle in the South, and the constant travel and personal appearances, his hectic schedule began to take its toll. At the age of forty-three, his hair was now fully gray, and he walked with difficulty. Within a year, he would require knee surgery and begin walking with a cane.

Around the time of Jackie's Hall of Fame induction, a new fast-food steakhouse, part of a chain, opened in Harlem. It was owned by a Jewish man, Sol Singer, who leased the store from the building's owner, another Jewish man named Frank Schiffman. Schiffman also owned the world-renowned Apollo Theater in Harlem, a showcase for black entertainers.

Local steakhouse owners worried that the chain's low prices would draw business away from their restaurants. Pickets soon appeared outside the new restaurant. The protest was organized and led by Lewis H. Michaux, owner of a black-themed bookstore and

In 1964, Jackie addresses the crowd at this civil-rights rally. He remained a vocal proponent of civil rights long after his baseball career ended.

leader of a black nationalist group called the Harlem Consumers Committee, that believed that African Americans should support one another and become independent from white society.

Many of the protesters carried anti-Semitic signs. Schiffman, who had long contributed to civil-rights groups and knew many of the black religious, community, and political leaders in Harlem, called on these leaders for help. They all refused, frightened to take a white man's side against a black-led protest.

Jackie wrote about the protest in his newspaper column condemning the anti-Semitic tone of the protesters. "Anti-Semitism is as rotten as anti-Negroism," he wrote, speaking as someone who abhorred bigotry no matter what form it took. Roy Wilkins sent Jackie a telegram supporting his views. In it, he wrote: "Negroes cannot use the slimy tools of anti-Semitism or indulge in racism, the very tactics against which we cry out. We are lost if we adopt [Ku Klux] Klan methods in the name of exalting black people." In response to Jackie's column, Michaux called for a boycott of the local Chock Full o' Nuts restaurant in Harlem and organized a rally to take place a few days later, at which Michaux and a controversial black Muslim leader named Malcolm X were scheduled to speak.

A local black radio station, WWRL, invited Robinson and

Jackie is shown here being interviewed at the March on Washington—a political rally where Dr. King recited his famous "I have a dream" speech—on August 28, 1963. His son David is at his side.

# Malcolm X

Born Malcolm Little in 1925 in Omaha, Nebraska, the man who would come to call himself Malcolm X was the son of a Baptist minister who was also an early civil-rights activist. In time, Malcolm would embrace the teachings of the Nation of Islam leader Elijah Muhammad. Muhammad believed that white society actively worked to stop African Americans from empowering themselves and reaching political, economic, and social gains. He preached black separatism, rather than working toward integration within what he called the white-controlled system.

Considering "Little" to be a slave name, Malcolm Little changed his name to Malcolm X. A break with Muhammad and a trip to Mecca in Saudi Arabia opened his eyes to sharing beliefs with and working with people of other races and cultures. Slowly, his views shifted toward the value of integration. But the controversial figure had already made many enemies within both the government and the Nation of Islam organization. On February 21, 1965, Malcolm X was shot dead by three gunmen, all members of the Nation of Islam.

Despite the fact that the two men had many disagreements, Jackie Robinson said of Malcolm X upon his death, "His murderers quieted his voice but clothed him in martyrdom and deepened his influence. In death Malcolm became larger than he had been in life."

This is a photograph of the only meeting between Martin Luther King, Jr. (left), and Malcolm X (right). It was on March 26, 1964, in Washington, D.C.

Michaux to debate the issue on the air. Shortly after the debate, Michaux asked his supporters to stop their protests at the steakhouse, the Chock Full o' Nuts, and the Apollo Theater. "I believe our debate had a healthy effect on the community and on black thinking," Jackie said. "It was a clear example of two people who were at terrible odds with each other resolving their problems through reason."

## Freedom National Bank

In 1964, two things led Jackie to leave his position at Chock Full o' Nuts. He believed that blacks could better control their fate if they began to own their own businesses. He viewed economic opportunities in black communities as a true example of black power, "from the standpoint of becoming a producer, a manufacturer, a developer and creator of business, a provider of jobs. For too long the Negro has been only the consumer." To this end, Jackie had been exploring several business opportunities, including starting the first black-owned bank in New York.

The second factor in Jackie's decision to leave Chock Full o' Nuts was the upcoming presidential race, in which he had decided to support New York Governor Nelson Rockefeller in the Republican primaries. Jackie still believed that blacks needed to have a voice in both political parties, and he once again chose to focus on the candidate rather than on the party. When Rockefeller offered Jackie a job as his deputy national director, Robinson gladly accepted.

He resigned from Chock Full o' Nuts. This change allowed him to earn a living supporting a politician in whom he believed, and it also left him time to help with the start-up of what would become the Freedom National Bank. His involvement with Rockefeller ultimately led to disappointment, as the more conservative Barry Goldwater, no supporter of civil rights, won the nomination to run as the Republican candidate in the presidential election. Goldwater lost the election to Democrat Lyndon B. Johnson.

Jackie's involvement with the Freedom National Bank was a much greater success. Teaming with Harlem businessmen who knew that Jackie's popularity and personality could open many doors, he worked hard to make the bank a reality.

"Freedom National is not just another local bank," Jackie, who was the bank's chairman of the board, said at its dedication in January 1965. "It is the determination of the Negro to become an integral part of the mainstream of our American economy."

The bank was a huge success. Within five years, it had become the biggest black-owned and -run bank in America. Finally, black people seeking loans to start new businesses in the black community had somewhere they could go where they would be treated fairly and not simply rejected because of the color of their skin.

*The bank was a huge success. Within five years, it had become the biggest black-owned and -run bank in America.*

Jackie was achieving success in the business world while remaining an active force in the civil-rights movement. His greatest challenges in the coming years would lie not at work or in the realm of politics or activism, but rather at home and with his own health.

# CHAPTER 11

# The Final Years

*A life is not important except in the impact it has on other lives.*

Changes were taking place in the Robinson home. In 1960, Rachel had earned a master's degree in psychiatric nursing. She planned to use her education once her children were old enough to be more independent. She also didn't want to go through her entire life only as Mrs. Jackie Robinson. She was an intelligent, independent person who wanted an identity of her own. In 1965, Rachel took a job as an assistant professor at the Yale University School of Nursing. She also worked as the director of nursing at a medical center in New Haven, Connecticut.

Things were also changing for Jackie and Rachel's oldest son, but not for the better. Jackie's relationship with Jackie Jr. had been troubled for a while. Jackie Jr. had difficulty growing up in the shadow of a famous and talented man. Having been given the same name as his superstar

Jackie poses outside his home in Connecticut in the 1960s.

father—something Jackie Sr. came to regret—didn't make things any easier for Jackie Jr.

As a teenager, Jackie Jr. ran away from home for a while, as an attempt to live away from the burden of being Jackie Robinson's son. Then, in 1964, he enlisted in the army. He was sent to fight in the Vietnam War, where in 1965 he was injured but chose to return to active duty.

Just as the Robinsons were coping with the news that their son had been injured in battle, word came of the death of Branch Rickey. At the funeral, Jackie said he felt "almost as if I had lost my own father." Having grown up without a father, Jackie viewed Rickey as a real father figure in his life. And he felt as if Rickey had treated him like a son.

## Nightmare, Recovery, and Tragedy

Jackie's own son was discharged from the army in June 1967. He returned home no more sure of his future or how to get out from under his father's shadow than he had been before he went into the service. Jackie Jr. spent little time at home, telling his parents that he had to figure out what he wanted to do with his life and that he needed to spend time away from them to do this. In reality, he was hiding something from his parents—his drug addiction, which began in Vietnam and worsened upon his return. Jackie and Rachel were shocked to learn of their son's drug problem.

Jackie Sr.'s own health was declining as well. His legs still ached and his eyesight was getting worse, the result of his continuing battle with diabetes, from which he had suffered for many years.

There were some bright spots during this difficult period of his life. The increase in the number of black voters in the South was encouraging. And the fact that southern politicians—who only a few years earlier had fought to keep blacks from voting—were now courting black voters was something Jackie called "a miracle." The reelection of Nelson Rockefeller as New York's governor, a campaign Jackie worked hard on, was also satisfying to him.

The year 1968 brought many heartaches not only to the Robinson family, but also to the entire nation. Politically, Jackie worked hard for Rockefeller's next bid for the presidency, only to be disappointed by his loss to Richard Nixon for the Republican nomination. Nixon would then go on to become president, defeating Hubert Humphrey, whom Jackie supported in the general election.

Jackie shakes hands with Nelson Rockefeller, the governor of New York, in 1967. Jackie worked on Rockefeller's bid for the Republican nomination for president in 1968, but the governor lost to Richard Nixon.

The assassinations of Dr. Martin Luther King, Jr., and Senator Robert Kennedy, President John F. Kennedy's brother and a big supporter of civil rights, stunned the nation. They affected Jackie as they affected all Americans, but they hit him as personal losses as well, since he knew and respected both men. That same year, his mother, Mallie Robinson, died at her home at 121 Pepper Street, the house in which Jackie and his siblings had grown up. Jackie himself suffered a mild heart attack that year to go along with his other physical ailments.

One nightmarish thread that ran through all of 1968 and beyond was the situation with Jackie Jr. In March, he was arrested on charges of possession of marijuana and heroin, and also possession of a gun. The whole family was shocked.

In the summer of 1968, Jackie Jr. entered the Daytop Rehabilitation Program, a drug **rehab clinic**, in Seymour, Connecticut. The family worried, and Jackie felt somewhat guilty for not having been closer to Jackie Jr. and for unintentionally putting pressure on his son to live up to his father's fame and ability. "I've had more effect on other people's kids than on my own," he said after Jackie Jr.'s arrest.

All Jackie wanted now was to get his son back, healed and healthy once again. Thanks to the people at Daytop, he got his wish. With Jackie Jr. well on the road to recovery, in May 1970, the Robinsons hosted a picnic at their home for members of Daytop. It was their way of saying thank-you. As the picnic ended, Jackie extended his hand to his son, unsure of what feelings Jackie Jr. still had toward him. Jackie Jr. pushed the hand aside, pulled his father close, and gave him a huge hug. "That single moment paid for every bit of sacrifice, every bit of anguish, I had ever undergone," Jackie later wrote. "I had my son back."

In November, Jackie Jr. graduated from Daytop and came home for good, healthy and happy. He had decided to join the staff at Daytop to use his experiences to help others in trouble. Jackie Sr. could not have been prouder of his son.

As 1971 began, Jackie Sr.'s health was continuing a steady decline. He now had heart and lung ailments along with the diabetes that continued to decrease his vision and make it more and more difficult to get around on legs that hurt or were numb.

*As the picnic ended, Jackie extended his hand to his son, unsure of what feelings Jackie Jr. still had toward him. Jackie Jr. pushed the hand aside, pulled his father close, and gave him a huge hug.*

Then, on June 17, 1971, early in the morning, the car Jackie Jr. was driving home on the Merritt Parkway in Connecticut spun out of control and crashed. He was killed instantly. The death stunned and shattered the family, overwhelming them with grief. Just as Jackie Jr. had finally found peace, health, and a strong bond with his family, he had been taken from them at the age of twenty-four.

An outpouring of love and support came from friends of the family and those who knew Jackie Jr. at Daytop, as well as from total strangers. Mostly, the family chose to be alone as a group, each one dealing with the terrible loss as they huddled together and supported one another.

## A Hero's Final Journey

The following year, on October 15, 1972, just before the second game of the World Series between the Cincinnati Reds and the Oakland A's at Riverfront Stadium in Cincinnati, Jackie

Jackie throws out the ceremonial first pitch before the Cincinnati Reds hosted the Oakland A's in a World Series game at Riverfront Stadium on October 15, 1972. It was the last public appearance for Jackie.

Robinson was honored on the twenty-fifth anniversary of his first season in Major League Baseball. Before heading out onto the field to speak to the crowd, in what would be his final public appearance, he ran into his former teammates Pee Wee Reese and Joe Black.

These longtime friends were shocked by what they saw. The once powerful, speedy warrior now walked with great difficulty—he had already scheduled an operation to have one of his legs amputated—and he was blind in one eye. "I'll take awhile and get an artificial leg, and I'll learn to walk and I'll play golf, and you know what, Pee Wee? I'll still beatcha'," Jackie said defiantly.

Then he strode onto a baseball field for the last time in his life to address the crowd. He told them how pleased he was to be there, and then, using his final opportunity to take a swipe at injustice, he added, "[but] I'm going to be tremendously more pleased and more proud when I look at that third base coaching line one day and see a black face managing in baseball." Then he turned and walked from the field and out of the public eye for the very last time.

Nine days later, on the morning of October 24, 1972, Jackie Robinson had a heart attack at his home in Stamford, Connecticut. He died in the ambulance on the way to the hospital at the age of fifty-three. The funeral was held at New York's Riverside Church on October 29. More than 2,500 mourners packed the cathedral. Thousands more gathered outside.

Governor Nelson Rockefeller was there, as were Roy Wilkins, head of the NAACP; New York City Mayor John Lindsay; baseball commissioner Bowie Kuhn; and, of course, former teammates and other athletes including Pee Wee Reese, Don Newcombe, Jim Gilliam, Carl Erskine, Roy Campanella, Joe Black, Ralph Branca, Larry Doby, Monte Irvin, Hank Aaron, Joe Louis, Bill Russell, and Hank Greenberg.

The Reverend Jesse Jackson, a good friend of the Robinson family, gave the eulogy, a stirring

The U.S. Post Office issued this commemorative stamp featuring Jackie in 1982.

tribute to Jackie in which he pointed out that death would not bring an end to the good work that he had done during his life. "No grave can hold that body down," he told the mourners, "because it belongs to the ages! He was the black knight and he checkmated bigotry!" Following the funeral service, the procession moved through Harlem, with a stop at the Freedom National Bank, then into Brooklyn on its way to Cypress Hills Cemetery, where Jackie Robinson was buried beside his son.

> "He was the black knight and he checkmated bigotry!"

Thousands of people lined every mile of the route, wanting a chance to say good-bye and pay their respects to their beloved hero. "If he had done nothing else in his life after 1947 [Jackie's first year in the majors], he would be entitled to be an American legend," Roy Wilkins said. But of course, Jackie Robinson did so much more. Along the way, he changed America for the better.

## The Legacy

Jackie Robinson's legacy is seen every time an African American player sets foot onto a Major League Baseball field and every time a black citizen of the United States votes. The Robinson family has worked very hard to keep his legacy alive. In 1973, one year after Jackie's death, Rachel Robinson started the Jackie Robinson Foundation, which provides college scholarships to poor and minority students.

On April 15, 1997, on the fiftieth anniversary of Jackie's first game, Major League Baseball retired his uniform number, 42, a great honor in baseball tradition, from all its teams. No team will ever assign that number to another player. Then in 2004, April 15 was designated Jackie Robinson Day in Major League

# The Jackie Robinson Foundation

The Jackie Robinson Foundation was founded by Rachel Robinson in 1973 as a tribute to her late husband's memory and his many achievements. The foundation's purpose is to help those students most in need of assistance to get a college education when they would not otherwise be able to afford one.

The foundation's Education and Leadership Development Program provides mentors for students, runs leadership workshops, helps place students into summer internships, and helps them find jobs. The result is much more than simply handing a student a check to pay tuition. The foundation believes in helping to create future leaders through its efforts and support. More than 1,200 students have been helped by the foundation to date.

Jackie teaches baseball fundamentals to youngsters, including his son Jackie Jr., in this photo from 1957. After Jackie Sr.'s death, the Jackie Robinson Foundation carried on Jackie's commitment to kids.

On April 15, 2007, Major League Baseball celebrated the sixtieth anniversary of Jackie's debut game. More than two hundred players, managers, and coaches wore his number, including these players at Dodger Stadium in Los Angeles, California.

Baseball. Every year on that date, all Major League Baseball teams now celebrate the man and his achievements.

Jackie's daughter, Sharon Robinson, as director of educational programming for Major League Baseball, created Breaking Barriers: In Sports, In Life, a character-education program for schools based on the nine values that formed the core of Jackie's life—courage, determination, teamwork, persistence, integrity, citizenship, justice, commitment, and excellence.

These nine values are now also inscribed in the Jackie Robinson Rotunda, the Ebbets Field–inspired entryway to the New York Mets' home stadium, Citi Field, which opened in 2009. The Mets picked up the legacy of National League baseball in New York, five years after the Dodgers and Giants moved to

California. Many former Brooklyn Dodgers fans adopted the Mets as their new team when they entered the league in 1962.

The rotunda, which fans walk past on their way into the stadium, also contains a large number 42 and photos of Jackie's life, as well as a quote from Jackie himself: "A life is not important except in the impact it has on other lives." This quote also adorns his gravestone. Using these, his own words, as a measure of success, Jackie Robinson's life was indeed a success beyond measure.

Jackie's wife, Rachel Robinson, speaks at the dedication of the Jackie Robinson Rotunda at Citi Field on April 15, 2009. Some of the nine values Jackie lived by can be seen inscribed on the walls, as well as photographs of the athlete.

# Glossary

**abolished**—removed or taken away.

**anti-Semitic**—bigotry and hatred directed at Jewish people.

**bag**—baseball slang for "base."

**baserunning**—the movement of players from one base to another, requiring good judgment and decision-making ability as well as running speed.

**batting average**—the number of hits a player gets divided by the number of at bats he has. Players with a batting average of .300 or higher are considered to be the top hitters in baseball.

**bigotry**—prejudice, racism, intolerance, hatred of a particular group.

**canteen**—the place on an army base where soldiers go to eat, drink, and socialize during time off.

**civil rights**—personal rights guaranteed and protected by the U.S. Constitution, such as freedom of speech and freedom from discrimination.

**court-martial**—a trial of someone in the military that is carried out by the military.

**defamation**—the act of insulting or making offensive remarks about a person or group.

**discrimination**—unfair or unequal treatment of a person or group because of one's race, religion, nationality, gender, or sexual orientation.

**double play**—a play in which two outs are made during one batter's time at bat.

**dugout**—the shelter on the side of the baseball field where team members wait while not playing.

**error**—in baseball, a mistake made by a fielder that leads to runners reaching base or scoring runs, when the play should have been an out.

**fielding percentage**—a baseball statistic that measures the frequency with which a fielder successfully completes plays that result in batters being out.

**freedom rider**—any civil-rights activist who rode interstate buses into segregated parts of the United States to test the 1946 Supreme Court decision *Irene Morgan v. Commonwealth of Virginia*, in which the court ruled that segregation in interstate transportation was unconstitutional.

**heyday**—most successful period of time.

**honorable discharge**—release of a soldier from military service with recognition that the soldier performed his or her duties properly.

**legacy**—something important that is left behind after a person's death.

**lynching**—the act of being executed, usually by hanging, without due process of law.

**Major League Baseball**—the organization of the highest level of North American professional baseball, which consists of two leagues: the National

League and the American League. The champion team from each of the two major leagues face off in the World Series at the end of each season.

**martyred**—victimized for one's beliefs.

**mentor**—an advisor, counselor, teacher, or guide. A mentor is usually an experienced, older person who helps a younger, inexperienced one.

**morale**—a group's feelings of togetherness and mutual support.

**plantation**—a farm on which many workers are used.

**RBI**—run or runs batted in. Whenever a batter's hit, walk, or sacrifice results in a run scoring, the batter is credited with an RBI.

**rehab clinic**—a place where people go to overcome their abuse of, or addiction to, alcohol and/or drugs.

**scholarships**—awards given to students to pay for their school fees.

**segregation**—the forced separation of people of different races, religions, nationalities, genders, or sexual orientation.

**sit-ins**—a form of nonviolent protest in which people sit down in a place, until they are removed by force, to bring attention to a cause or an injustice.

**stealing**—in baseball, when a runner on base runs to the next base as the pitcher starts to throw his pitch, rather than waiting until the batter has hit the ball.

# Bibliography

**Books**

Falkner, David. *Great Time Coming*. New York: Touchstone, 1996.

Greenberg, Hank. *Hank Greenberg: The Story of My Life*. New York: Times Books, 1989.

Long, Michael G. *First Class Citizenship: The Civil Rights Letters of Jackie Robinson*. New York: Holt Paperbacks, 2008.

Rampersand, Arnold. *Jackie Robinson, A Biography*. New York: Ballantine Books, 1997.

Robinson, Jackie. *I Never Had It Made*. New York: Ecco/HarperCollins Publishers, 1995.

Robinson, Rachel. *Jackie Robinson: An Intimate Portrait*. New York: Harry N. Abrams, 1996.

Robinson, Sharon. *Jackie's Nine: Jackie Robinson's Values to Live By*. New York: Scholastic Paperbacks, 2002.

———. *Promises to Keep: How Jackie Robinson Changed America*. New York: Scholastic Press, 2004.

———. *Stealing Home*. New York: HarperCollins Publishers, 1996.

Simon, Scott. *Jackie Robinson and the Integration of Baseball*. Hoboken, N.J.: John Wiley & Sons, 2002.

Tygiel, Jules. *Baseball's Great Experiment: Jackie Robinson and His Legacy (25th Anniversary Edition)*. New York: Oxford University Press, 2008.

**Web Sites**

Barton, Leonard G. "The Pearl Harbor Day Page," *The Contra Costa Demonstrator*. http://www.ccdemo.info/PearlHarbor/PearlHarborDayRemembered.html.

"Bobby Thomson launches 'The Shot Heard 'Round The World' & 'The Giants Win The Pennant!'," MLB.com, October 3, 1951. http://mlb.mlb.com/ mlb/baseballs_best/mlb_bb_gamepage.jsp?story_page=bb_51reg_100351_ bknnyg.

"Jackie Robinson," Library of Congress. http://www.loc.gov/topics/baseball/ featured/jackierobinson.html

The Jackie Robinson Foundation. www.jackierobinson.org.

"Jackie Robinson Quotes," Baseball Almanac.com. http://www.baseball-almanac.com/quotes/quojckr.shtml

McKeeby, David. "End of U.S. Military Segregation Set Stage for Rights Movement," February 25, 2008. http://www.america.gov/st/diversity-english/2008/February/20080225120859liameruoy0.9820215.html.

Mission Statement of the Anti-Defamation League, October 1913. http:// www.adl.org/about.asp.

"Red Barber," *Brittanica Online Encyclopedia*, 2009. http://www.britannica.com/ EBchecked/topic/52846/Red-Barber.

Robinson, Jackie. "Pro Baseball Hall of Fame Induction Address," July 23, 1962. http://www.americanrhetoric.com/speeches/ jackierobinsonbaseballhofinduction.htm.

"Standing Up for Freedom," Academy of Achievement, October 2005. http://www.achievement.org/autodoc/page/par0bio-1.

"Sportscasters: Red Barber," Radio Hall of Fame. http://www.radiohof.org/ sportscasters/redbarber.html

# Source Notes

The following citations list the sources of quoted material in this book. The first and last few words of each quotation are cited and followed by their source. Complete information referenced sources can be found in the Bibliography.

**Abbreviations:**

Here's the list of quotes and sources:

**ADL**—Mission Statement of the ADL

**AM**—"End of U.S. Military Segregation Set Stage for Rights Movement"

**PAGE 72** *"I have no. . . . cheek to insults."*: INH, p. 80

**PAGE 73** *"As long as. . . . troublemaker, a sorehead."*: INH, p. 79

**PAGE 75** *"to stop the . . . treatment to all."*: ADL

**PAGE 77** *"O'Malley's attitude . . . viciously [hostile]."*: INH, p. 92

**PAGE 77** *"It has been . . . members of our race."*: JR, p. 231

**PAGE 77** *"Sometimes my. . . . all respected Jackie."*: JR, p. 231

**PAGE 77** *"There was never . . . judgment than Jackie."*: JAQ

## CHAPTER 8: Champions at Last

**PAGE 78** *"Wait 'til next year!"*: INH, p. 120

**PAGE 80** *"The Giants win . . . the pennant!"*: BT

## CHAPTER 9: Endings and Beginnings

**PAGE 85** *"The way I. . . . much for it."*: INH, p. 122

**PAGE 85** *"It's up to. . . . play for them."*: JR, p. 285

**PAGE 86** *"I remember . . . would burn down."*: SUF

**PAGE 87** *"The more I . . . are doing."*: JR, p. 287

**PAGE 92** *"The way I. . . . much for it."*: INH, p. 122

**PAGE 92** *"I can't help . . . year or two."*: JR, p. 308

## CHAPTER 10: Life After Baseball

**PAGE 93** *"Baseball was. . . . that was it."*: JR, p. 314

**PAGE 94** *"prepare this famous . . . rights spokesman."*: INH, p. 127

**PAGE 95** *"ensured that Negro . . . by the Constitution."*: GTC, p. 262

**PAGES 95–96** *"I have the. . . . of all Americans."*: JR, p. 323

**PAGE 97** *"I feel so. . . . happen to you."*: GTC, p. 290

**PAGE 99** *"a hero of . . . for every American."*: JR, p. 6

**PAGE 99** *"He has the. . . . honor him tonight."*: JR, p. 7

**PAGE 100** *"Today, it . . . is complete."*: IA

**PAGE 101** *"Anti-Semitism is as rotten as anti-Negroism,"*: JR, p. 365

**PAGE 101** *"Negroes cannot use. . . . exalting black people."*: INH, p. 148

**PAGE 102** *"His murderers quieted. . . . been in life."*: INH, p. 182

**PAGE 103** *"I believe our. . . . problems through reason."*: INH, p. 150

**PAGE 103** *"from the standpoint. . . . only the consumer."*: JR, p. 392

**PAGE 104** *"Freedom National. . . . our American economy."*: JR, p. 394

## CHAPTER 11: The Final Years

**PAGE 105** *"A life is . . . on other lives."*: JRF

**PAGE 106** *"almost as if I had lost my own father."*: JR, p. 403

**PAGE 107** *"a miracle."*: JR, p. 403

**PAGE 108** *"I've had more . . . on my own."*: JR, p. 423

**PAGE 108** *"That single moment. . . . my son back."*: INH, p. 226

**PAGE 110** *"I'll take awhile. . . . I'll still beatcha', "*: GTC, p. 342

**PAGE 111** *"[but] I'm going to . . . managing in baseball."*: JR, p. 459

**PAGE 112** *"No grave can. . . . checkmated bigotry!"*: GTC, pp. 344–345

**PAGE 112** *"He was the . . . checkmated bigotry!"*: GTC, pp. 344–345

**PAGE 112** *"If he had . . . an American legend,"*: GTC, p. 350

**PAGE 115** *"A life is . . . on other lives."*: JRF

# Image Credits

# About the Author

**Michael Teitelbaum** has been a writer and editor of children's books and magazines for more than twenty years. He was editor of *Little League Magazine for Kids* and *Spider-Man Magazine*, which he created and edited for Marvel Entertainment. Michael is the author of a two-volume encyclopedia on the National Baseball Hall of Fame, published by Grolier, and was the writer/project editor of Breaking Barriers: In Sports, In Life, a character-education program based on the life of Jackie Robinson, created in association with Major League Baseball for Scholastic, Inc.

His other nonfiction writing includes books on sports history, women in sports, Chinese immigration, the history of radio and television, and how comic books are made.

Michael's fiction includes books based on popular characters such as Spider-Man, Superman, Batman, Garfield, and Kermit the Frog. His latest fiction includes *The Scary States of America*, published by Delacorte, and *Backyard Sports*, published by Grosset & Dunlap. The opportunity to write a biography of Jackie Robinson, one of Michael's heroes, was a dream come true.

Michael and his wife, Sheleigh, split their time between New York City and their 170-year-old farmhouse in the Catskill Mountains of upstate New York.

# Index